The Writer's Relief Field Guide To Literary Agents

Find, Attract, Keep, And Manage Your Dream Agent

by

Writer's Relief, Inc.

Helping writers prepare and target their submissions since 1994

Table Of Contents

Part Four: After Submitting... What Happens Next?

Part Five: Trouble In Paradise

Part Six: Special Considerations

Bonus Section: Build Your Author Platform

Introduction: Who We Are And Why You Should Listen To Us

Writer's Relief is an author's submission service, and we've been helping creative writers make submissions since 1994. We're a highly specialized service with expert knowledge of the publishing industry.

We help book authors find literary agents.

We help poetry, short story, and essay writers get published in literary journals.

Our work is personalized, careful, and precise—we're not a "submission factory" and do not support any kind of submission spam. We love writers, and it's our goal to see our clients get published. That means we take a personal, hands-on approach to helping our clients make submissions.

We also do a fair amount of congratulating, advising, strategizing, encouraging, consoling, and cheering on. We have seen countless clients connect with reputable, talented literary agents over the years. We've also helped our clients answer many of the tough questions that can arise, such as:

- Do I even need a literary agent?
- What are the warning signs of a bad literary agent? How do I find a good one?
- How long do I wait before I follow up with an agent?
- How do I get my agent to pay more attention to me?
- What can I do to make my pitch stand out?
- What should I do when a literary agent asks for an exclusive?
- How do I get an agent for my self-published book?
- Can I submit my revised book to agents who saw it already? How?

Now, after many years of offering our expertise to the writers on our very limited and exclusive client list, we have decided to pass our expert advice along to you.

How Is This Book Different From Every Other Book About Literary Agents?

This is NOT a book about writing query letters. There are many books about query letter writing—you can even check out our own fantastic query letter book by visiting the Writer's Relief website. While this book touches on query letter basics, advanced query writing strategies are *not* what we are focusing on here.

This is NOT a market book filled with specific listings of literary agencies. There are plenty of those already. Plus, our private database is overflowing with itemized notes on the preferences of literary agents gleaned from their many personal comments to our clients since 1994. We couldn't fit all our detailed listings in a book even if we wanted to!

This is a book about how to create a successful relationship with the RIGHT literary agent for your career.

The advice in this book addresses many situations authors face—whether you are a new writer who doesn't really understand how literary agents work and is afraid of being scammed; or whether you are a veteran writer trying to figure out how to get more attention from your literary agent or how to let your agent go.

Who Is This Book For?

This book is best for writers who would like to get a traditional (paying) publisher for their book by working with a literary agent. If you self-published a book and are now looking for an agent, you will find lots of helpful information here.

You may notice a certain amount of "quiet repetition" throughout this book. We want to assure you that this is intentional. Later, when you refer back to this book again when dealing with submission issues, you'll be able to find the information that you're looking for in a natural and organic way—instead of hunting and pecking for it throughout the whole book. Also, we all know that some repetition helps ideas "stick" without the need for annoying memorization.

Trust Your Instincts

If you read enough about the publishing industry, or if you attend enough writing conferences, you will know that there are conflicting opinions about a lot of the topics we cover in this book. Everyone has his or her own idea about what's best.

What we offer readers is a perspective that is uniquely pro-writer (as opposed to pro-agent or pro-editor). While you may not agree with all of our recommendations, we hope we can offer food for thought. Ultimately, you must make your own way within the publishing industry using your instincts as your guide.

We've been working with writers for many years, and it's always a thrill when one of our clients calls us to say, "I got a literary agent!" We would not mislead our clients and say that getting a literary agent is easy and straightforward. But we do know that our expert, personalized targeting connects our clients with the literary agents who are most likely to enjoy their writing. And we know that our clients' queries and proposals go out into the world in the best possible shape. We love writers and are proud of the work we do!

If you're interested in finding out how Writer's Relief can help you (we can manage as much or as little of the submission process as you like), just find us online or give us a call. We're easy to reach.

But, of course, you do not *need* a Writer's Relief submission strategist managing your submissions to literary agents in order to succeed. If you've got the energy, dedication, focus, and time for making submissions, you'll be fine.

For now, just enjoy this book. We hope it will answer your questions about finding, obtaining, and dealing with literary agents.

Please contact us and let us know what you think! We would love to hear your story about getting or working with a literary agent. We might even use it on our blog!

Happy reading!

Ronnie L. Smith

Ronnie L. Smith, President
Writer's Relief, Inc.
(866) 405-3003
www.WritersRelief.com

Part One

Welcome To The World Of Literary Agents

Who They Are, What They Do, And What They Mean To You

What Agents Will And Will Not Do For Writers

Finding a good literary agent is the first step in getting your novel or book project into the hands of a traditional (advance-paying) publisher.

A literary agent is the middleman between you and potential publishers—your best hope for getting your book published. But what does a literary agent actually do for a writer? And what don't they do?

What Kinds Of Writers Need A Literary Agent?

If you want a traditional book deal and you are writing in the following genres, then you may want to seek the help of a literary agent.

- Full-length novels (fiction) of all genres
- Memoirs
- Self-help and how-to (prescriptive nonfiction)
- Collections of short stories and essays
- Self-published authors who want a traditional book deal

What Literary Agents Do

1. A literary agent's top job is to find an editor who likes your book enough to buy it. Reputable literary agents have a wide network of contacts and relationships with acquisition editors at publishing houses. They know what editors are looking for, and they're experts at sending your work to the right people. Because editors know that submissions from literary agents have already made it through a stringent screening process, agented submissions usually go to the top of the pile.

Literary agents will NOT purchase the rights to your book and then turn around and try to sell your book to publishers. Nor can they promise to sell your book.

2. Literary agents pitch your book project to publishers and try to get you the best deal. It is in their best interest to negotiate lucrative contracts with publishers, since literary agents work on commission. They also manage your business affairs with the publisher once the deal goes through—contract disputes, royalty statements, collecting money, cover art issues, etc.—keeping you on good terms with the editor and freeing up your time to write.

Literary agents are NOT always attorneys, but they do specialize in book contracts and are well versed in authors' rights.

3. A good literary agent will often edit or critique a manuscript and offer valuable suggestions to increase its marketability. BUT you should never query (aka reach out to) an agent unless you have a completed, professionally formatted, and carefully proofread novel or memoir in hand. (Only prescriptive nonfiction, such as how-to or self-help books, can be pitched without having been finished.)

Literary agents do NOT offer line-by-line edits or make rewrites. It's up to the writer to incorporate the agent's suggested changes. Agents are not interested in helping you master the art of writing. Their focus is on the business of writing.

4. Literary agents are authors' advocates. They don't make money unless you make money, so their goal is to get you the best deal. Most reputable agents will make a commission. They offer encouragement and support and help keep you on track with deadlines and rewrites. They can also help shape your career by suggesting new ideas, finding wider audiences, and keeping you abreast of changes and trends in the publishing industry.

Literary agents are NOT tax consultants, publicists, personal bankers, or writing coaches. They often offer moral support, but they are not interested in being your therapist. They will not handle your advertising and marketing. And they're certainly not interested in being your personal answering service.

It's up to the writer to take advantage of all the services a good literary agent can offer. As an author's ally, a good literary agent can make a writer's life more successful and rewarding.

What's The Difference Between An Agent And An Editor?

Literary agents and editors have different but important roles in the book publishing industry. Many writers wonder: Can you get an editor without a literary agent? Do you need a literary agent to get a book published? Why have both a literary agent and an editor—isn't one or the other enough?

What is the point of having a literary agent? Major publishing houses will not consider your book unless a literary agent submits it on your behalf.

What is the point of having an editor? At most major publishing houses, an editor's work is to acquire strong book projects and make those book projects even stronger through critique.

Who pays a literary agent? You do. We will explain more on this later.

Who pays the editor? An editor is generally an employee of a publishing house. A writer and editor are both paid by the publisher for their work; however, editors are often charged with determining how much a writer is paid.

Will a literary agent critique your book? Yes and no. A literary agent's primary job is NOT to offer editorial advice on a book; an agent's task is to sell a book to an editor. Sometimes a literary agent will offer editorial guidance for a book, but it's not mandatory.

Will an editor critique your book? Yes, an editor will critique a book. Editors work closely with authors to make sure a book is ready for a large audience and public scrutiny.

How does a writer get a literary agent? Typically, a writer can get a literary agent by composing one-page query letters and sending submissions via email and mail.

How does a writer get an editor at a publishing house? A writer can get an editor by having his/her literary agent pitch a manuscript to editors. In other words, a writer doesn't query an editor directly. Some editors at independent publishing houses do accept queries from unagented (unrepresented) authors. But generally, major publishers do not.

How Writer's Relief Fits In

Writer's Relief is neither a literary agency nor a publishing house that employs editors. Writer's Relief manages the submission process for writers who wish to submit their work to literary agents. We do not work based on commission: Like most specialized secretarial services, our work is based on flat fees. Visit our website to learn more.

How Literary Agents Get Paid: Standard Commission Practices And Payments

The standard industry practice is that literary agents do not get paid for their work except through the commission they make when they sell your book. As a client, you may be required to pay for the cost of making phone calls and mailing packages. But otherwise, a literary agent is paid through commission.

Standard Commission On Book Sales To Domestic Publishers

Generally speaking, literary agents receive 15% of your total income from the first sale of the book before taxes. If you are paid a $10,000 "advance" on the sale of the book to a major publisher, your literary agent will take a commission of $1,500. If you make any royalties beyond your advance, your agent will receive 15% of those royalties. Some literary agents have been known to take higher or lower commissions, but most take 15%.

Commission On Foreign Subsidiary Rights And Translations

Literary agents tend to receive a 20% commission on foreign rights sales or translations. What this 20% commission actually means to you depends on your book contract and your literary agent contract. Let's consider two possible scenarios.

Scenario number one: Let's say your publisher has retained the right to license translations on your behalf to other publishers around the world. And now, let's say a publisher in France has decided to pay your American publisher for the right to create and sell a French translation. You keep half of that payment; the other half goes to your publisher.

But wait! What does your agent get out of it? Your literary agent will most likely take a 20% commission on the amount you receive from your publisher. So while you were paid half of the total contracted payment, your agent will receive 20% of *your* half.

Scenario number two: If your literary agent has retained your translation rights (so that he or she can find publishers around the world, instead of allowing the publisher to do it), your agent will still take 20% of the amount you are paid. Because many literary agencies have subsidiary partners in other countries to help them sell translation rights, it is likely that your literary agent will split the commission: Your literary agent keeps 10% and the foreign rights subsidiary agent keeps the other 10%.

Literary Agent Commission On Film Rights, Calendar Rights, And Audio Rights

Most literary agents will continue to take a 15% commission on whatever payment you receive.

Self-Publishing Literary Agent Commission

Some literary agents are beginning to help their clients self-publish their books—for a fee. We will explain more about this practice in an upcoming section. In exchange for the literary agency taking on the work of self-publishing a book on behalf of the client, the literary agency may take a commission of 15% on all sales. However, this is new territory at the time of this writing, so there are no current industry standards in place for this practice.

If Your Literary Agent Charges A Commission That Is Not Standard

If you are considering signing up with a literary agent who is taking a commission outside of the industry standard, we recommend that you proceed with caution. We'll show you how to check out your potential literary agent further on in this book. For now, let's continue with our overview.

Paths To Publishing: What Kinds Of Publishers Are Available To You?

Let's review the various types of publishing companies that are out there. You will need to understand the difference between these publishers even if you decide to work with a literary agent.

What is a commercial or traditional publisher?

Literary agents primarily work with traditional publishers. These are the "household name" publishers, and they are highly selective. There are no costs to the author for printing, artwork, or distribution, and authors are paid up front for their books. Authors do need to be represented by a literary agent and do maintain the ownership of their work. Traditional publishers include Penguin Random House, Hachette Book Group, etc.

What is considered self-publishing?

All types of publishing in which the author assumes the majority of the financial risk can be deemed "self-publishing." But there are distinctions within the larger umbrella of self-publishing.

Historically, the term "self-publisher" referred to an author who started his or her own publishing company, paid ALL the costs of printing, and was responsible for marketing, distribution, promotion, etc. This is the equivalent of starting a publishing house. Authors who self-publish via their own publishing houses are not considered to be "traditionally" published.

Today, many self-publishing companies exist to help authors with the process of publishing their own books. In lieu of the writer starting his or her own company to handle cover art, copywriting, proofreading, and distribution, a self-publishing company handles all of these elements on the writer's behalf.

POD publishing:

POD stands for print on demand. POD publishers are self-publishing companies that can prepare and print your book—as few as two or as many as 2,000. POD publishers are generally self-publishing companies.

Vanity publishing:

This term is sometimes synonymous with self-publishing. A "vanity" publisher prints books at the author's expense. NOTE: The term "vanity" publisher" is sometimes considered pejorative, vague, and outdated by many people in the larger publishing industry; use it carefully or not at all.

Subsidy publishing:

This type of publisher shares the cost of (or subsidizes) publishing a book. Subsidy publishers are often selective, and the completed books belong to the publisher, NOT the author. The books remain in the publisher's possession until they are sold. Authors can collect royalties. Subsidy publishers are NOT generally considered traditional publishers, since the author bears part of the cost of publication.

Why Querying Literary Agents First Is Often Your Best Bet

There are many paths to publishing these days—through online e-presses, self-publishing, print on demand, and independent or university-affiliated publishing houses. But most of the writers who come to Writer's Relief dream of being among the small percentage of authors who publish their book with the "big-time" traditional publishing houses.

In spite of the many changes throughout the industry over the last decade, we believe that querying a literary agent remains the best first step in your quest to publish a book.

Agents And Editors: Let's Do Lunch

The roles of agents and editors are mutually beneficial. Literary agents are the front line in the submission process. They "weed out" the projects that they don't feel will be a good fit for publishers and try to save publishers' valuable time. Also, agents get to know the editors they submit to; they become familiar with their tastes and preferences. When an editor receives a manuscript recommendation from an agent she or he trusts, it's not much different than if you were to receive a book recommendation from a good friend.

So, What Are The Benefits Of Querying Agents First?

Here are just a few reasons we advocate getting a literary agent for book-length projects.

Foot in the door. The facts are plain: The vast majority of traditional publishing houses will not take you seriously—they won't even look at your work—unless you have an agent. If you're considering publishing with a smaller, independent publishing house, you may have a chance to get your manuscript reviewed without having an agent (but you'll be on your own with the contracts and negotiations).

If you're shooting for that pie-in-the-sky contract, an agent is the first, best step in getting you one. True—you can try self-publishing first to see if your book takes off. But the hard fact is that most self-published books barely make back the money that was put into them. And if your self-published book did not sell very well, it could harm more than help. So it's best to approach agents while you have a fresh new manuscript that has never been seen.

Effectiveness. Pitching your book to one agent is like pitching your book to dozens of editors. When an agent receives your submission, he or she reads it with an eye toward the editors who might like to buy it. A good agent will be running through his mental contacts list while reviewing your submission.

Author's protection. Sending out your manuscript with an agent means that someone is in your corner. Agents will negotiate contracts and tactfully intervene if the art department puts a naked centaur on your story about 19th-century Harlem. Having an agent means you might have more control over your work.

More money. If you are able to get a book deal, your agent will be able to negotiate your advance, your percentages on royalties, and more.

Subtext. If you approach a publishing house through an agency, your work will be taken more seriously. Having your name on an agent's letterhead goes a long way toward ensuring that publishers give your book a good read.

But What About All The People Who Get Book Deals Without An Agent?

You may have heard stories of self-published authors who landed a book deal after hand-selling their novel one copy at a time. You also may have heard stories of writers who land a big publisher through their blog.

But the reason you've heard those stories is because they are *exceptions*, not the norm. A far greater number of authors get book contracts the traditional way—by gaining agency representation before seeking a publisher.

What Can Go Wrong Without An Agent?

Literary agents aren't perfect. They're not superheroes. However literary agents—good ones—can make a HUGE difference in a writer's career. But what if a writer doesn't have (or want) one? What if a writer would rather keep the 15% commission that agents take for their services?

While we don't want to run around like Chicken Little and shout, "The sky is falling, the sky is falling," we do want to make it clear that literary agents can be worth what they're paid.

Here's A List Of Things That Can Go Wrong When A Writer Doesn't Have A Literary Agent

Your publisher acquires more rights than you are willing to give (or, your contract stinks). Unless you hire an intellectual property lawyer who knows the publishing business, not having an agent might cause serious harm when it's time to sign a book deal contract.

For example, suppose your contract indicates that your rights revert to you when fewer than 100 copies a year are sold. What types of books are we referring to here? Your digital books might sell 101 copies a year for the next fifty years—and you'll be stuck, even if you suspect you could make more money on the book if you were able to get the rights back and self-publish it. A good agent has your future in mind.

Your publisher lowballs your book deal. As much as you want to think that your editor is your friend, it's almost always going to be in an editor's best interest to acquire a book by offering as little money as possible. And that's bad for you.
Agents are trained negotiators; they know the going rates, and they help ensure your book gets the advance it's worth. Case in point: If you hire a general lawyer who looks at your contract and decides your 15% royalty rate is fine, you'll never know that 25% is the current industry standard.

You have to play the bad cop and the good cop at the same time. Writers who have agents have the distinct advantage of getting to play the "good cop" when things get sticky; the agent can do the table pounding and the pointed interrogation.

When the arguing and haggling are over, the writer's relationship with the editor is left intact—which is hugely important. If you don't have an agent, you have to be your own bad cop. You have to talk tough and say the things you don't want to say—the things that might damage your long-term relationship.

You could miss out on foreign rights sales. Some agents have strong foreign rights departments, which means they can nab deals to get your book translated into other languages. Some publishing houses will do this for you too; but if your publisher isn't aggressive about foreign book sales and translations, you'll need an agent to seek that additional income on your behalf.

You have to negotiate your own option. Most publishers have an option clause, giving them a kind of "right of first refusal" for your next book. But what if working with your publisher didn't go as smoothly as you'd hoped? It may take some fancy footwork, diplomacy, and timing to negotiate your way out of option territory and into a land where you can obtain another (better) book deal.

Do Self-Published Authors Need Literary Agents?

Back in the early days of self-publishing, it was generally held that book authors who were primarily interested in self-publishing did not need a literary agent.

Many self-published authors choose to publish their books on their own because they want to keep a larger percentage of their royalties.

But something interesting is starting to happen more and more in the publishing industry.

Literary agents are increasingly willing to work with authors who prefer to self-publish—and who have little or no interest in traditional publishing at all.

This is not a widespread trend yet, but it is something to watch.

What Do Literary Agents Have To Do With Self-Publishing?

Most of the time, literary agents will represent a self-published book in hopes that one day they can take that book and pitch it to a major New York publisher. Then, the literary agent will earn a standard 15% commission on the sale.

However, these days many writers don't necessarily *want* their book to be released by a major publisher. They believe that they will make more money if they publish a book themselves.

(Important Note: Writers who tend to take this position in a realistic way are often multi-published authors or writers who already have an established readership. On average, a self-published book by a new author might only sell a few hundred copies.)

Because so many established writers are requesting help with self-publishing, literary agents are adjusting their business models to accommodate the needs of their clients. Some literary agencies are willing to manage the writer's self-publishing efforts.

Not *every* literary agency is willing to help a writer with self-publishing. Most still do not. Those that do help writers self-publish their books take a commission for the work that they perform. At the moment, literary agents who help clients self-publish a book will often take 15% of the profits to cover their time spent performing the services that get the book on the shelves.

If there are up-front publishing costs, it may be the author who pays those costs, or it may be the agent, or it may be a split. Both literary agent and author are banking on the success of the book.

Some publishing companies do not require an author to put down a lot of money in the beginning. In these cases, a literary agent will simply take a 15% commission on any sales.

To sum up: A writer gives 15% of his or her profits to the literary agency, and in return the agent handles all of the details regarding self-publishing.

Here Are Some Of The Services A Literary Agent Might Perform For A Writer Who Wants To Self-Publish

- Review all contracts and modify them when possible

- Handle the administrative work involved in self-publishing

- Employ the right third-party professionals for cover art, copyediting, proofreading, etc.

- Help the author make connections that he or she couldn't make alone; we have heard from literary agents who have suggested that their relationships with the marketing departments at major book retailers help their clients' books get the spotlight

- Assist the author in transitioning from self-published to traditionally published—if the author decides that's what he or she wants to do. The agent will have intimate knowledge of the writer's history and be able to negotiate a great deal.

Is It Worthwhile To Ask An Agent To Handle Your Self-Publishing Efforts?

For some writers, having an agent manage all of their self-publishing efforts works out great: It means they don't have to do any of the hard work involved with publishing. They can focus on their writing. If you want help self-publishing and don't mind sharing your profits, you might want to consider querying agencies that offer support with self-publishing.

Other authors who are self-published can be quite vocal against the new business model: Why pay an agent 15% of profits when you can do all the work involved in self-publishing by yourself?

If you send out a query letter and a literary agent wants to talk about representing you, be sure you mention any future interest in self-publishing if you think that is the direction your career might go. Also, be aware of what it means if your literary agent offers to act as your publisher (as opposed to an assistant who helps *you* self-publish). You'll read more about that in a later section.

How Much Money Can You Make On A Book Deal?

"Writing is the only profession where no one considers you ridiculous if you earn no money."
—Jules Renard

How much money you can make on a book depends on many factors: the market for your writing, the strength of your voice and perspective, the timeliness of your topic, etc.

In the larger traditional publishing houses, writers receive what is called an "advance" for payment. This advance is a lump sum that acts as an advance against future royalties. Once the author has "earned out" his or her advance, then he or she can begin collecting any additional royalties.

A new writer may expect a publisher to pay anywhere from $2,000 and up for a book. A small book deal may be $5,000 to $20,000. A midrange deal may be $20,000 to $60,000. A significant deal may be $60,000 to $150,000. And, of course, advances can go through the roof for a book that every publisher wants.

Some smaller, independent houses may pay less than $2,000, especially for new writers or for books that may not have a wide appeal. (NOTE: These numbers are approximations, since there are no "rules" that dictate what is considered a big or small book deal.) Ultimately, the size of your book advance depends on the excitement surrounding your book and the size of the editor's budget. A good literary agent can help you negotiate the best deal.

Along with traditional publishers, there are new publishing models forming. Some publishers—who have national distribution, best-selling authors, and strong sales—are foregoing traditional advances. Instead of paying their writers one lump sum of money at the beginning and then relatively small royalties later on, they are instead offering authors a higher share of royalties from the start—with no advance.

If you are self-publishing, how much money you make on your book depends on how much effort you're willing to put into promoting it and how strong your book is.

How Long Does It Take To Find An Agent And Get A Book Published?

To make it as a writer, you must prepare to be patient.

As you may already know, it can take years to write a good book.

Once you start the process of finding a literary agent to represent your book, you could be looking at another few months to a year of making submissions.

Then, your literary agent will begin submitting your book to editors. The best literary agents will begin submitting your book very shortly after they receive it from you. Other literary agents might need to put your book in a queue, sending books out to editors in the order that they were received.

The process of submitting your book to an editor through a literary agency could take anywhere from a couple of months (for a book that everyone is very excited about) to a year or more.

If your book is selected for publication, it can take months to draw up and agree upon a contract, then weeks for the accounting department to write your check (which goes to your agent, who must process it before you see it).

Some publishers stipulate that they have up to two years to publish a project from the date a contract is signed.

Then, finally, after a long and exciting journey, your book comes out!

Remember, you don't need to be on *The New York Times* list tomorrow (and you probably won't). Enjoy the experience of being a writer. You've earned the right to be proud of all your hard work and perseverance. With the right amount of patience, focus, and talent, success is within your grasp.

Does A Poet Need A Literary Agent?

But What About Poetry?

Until you've reached the level of "rock star" poet, seeking a literary agent to represent your writing might be something of a waste of time—for you and for agents. Here's why.

Reasons Poets Tend Not To Get Literary Agents

Money talks. As you know, literary agents are paid on commission. So the only kinds of books they're interested in are, let's face it, books that make money. Poetry books, for the most part, tend not to be giant moneymakers.

That said, we don't want to decry literary agents as money-hungry salespeople who'll do anything for a buck. Good literary agents have to love the projects they represent. Many literary agents will represent "high" literary fiction even though such novels don't always sell in quite the same numbers as commercial fiction.

But in general, reputable agents aren't interested in representing books of poems. It's not that they dislike poetry. It's about being practical.

Independent presses rule. Most of the best poetry today is being published by independent presses. And if you want your book of poems published, an indie publisher may be your best bet. Independent publishers work from various models: Some pay a traditional advance, others absorb the cost of production but pay some royalties, and others split the cost of publication and share the profits too.

Many independent presses are highly regarded for publishing quality work, and some poets do very well with them. But a poet doesn't necessarily need a literary agent to represent his or her work with indie publishers. Poets can submit their work for consideration without a literary agent, and a lawyer can review contract language to ensure the writer is protected.

Self-publishing. The great news for poets is that self-publishing is more accessible (and possibly more affordable) than it's ever been before. Whether you want to publish your poetry collection in print or online, there's a self-publishing company that can help.

Writers who self-publish their poetry collection can benefit from keeping more of their own royalties. So if you're giving readings and talks, you can hold on to more of the proceeds from your sales.

Let's Dream Of A Future...

We at Writer's Relief like to imagine the day when poets (and books of poems) are in such high demand that literary agents clamor to represent them and offer poets big, fat book deals.

But until that day comes, remember that being knowledgeable about the poetry publication process, asking a lot of questions, and engaging a lawyer might be as much help as you need.

Part Two

Get Ready To Get A Literary Agent

Preparing The Perfect Pitch

Prepare For Success BEFORE You Start Querying Literary Agents

The most important factor in getting a good literary agent to represent you is a well-written book. No other part of the process is as vital as this one key element:

If you want to get a great agent, write a great book.

That said, there are strategic steps you can take as you prepare to start your queries that can help ensure your book rises to the top of the slush pile.

Submission Strategy Step #1: Get Some Publishing Credentials If You Can

Submission Strategy Step #2: Know Your Book Genre Inside And Out

Submission Strategy Step #3: Write A Strong Query Letter

Submission Strategy Step #4: Tackle The Tough Job Of Writing Your Synopsis

Submission Strategy Step #5: Prepare Your Opening Pages

Submission Strategy Step #1:
Get Some Publishing Credentials If You Can

If you're a writer whose dream is to land a publishing contract and see your book in stores nationwide, consider creating a strong writing bio first. Building publication credits before querying a literary agent is a strategy that gets your foot in the door. Based on our years of experience preparing submissions, writers who can boast publications of shorter works tend to have an easier time getting an agent's interest.

Build your publication credits by submitting short stories, poems, or essays to literary journals. Or send your commentaries and articles to magazines.

Some folks believe it's not important to have published any short works before approaching an agent. With a fantastic novel that can stand on its own, you may well be able to find an agent without any publication credentials at all. However, there are a number of reasons why publishing your shorter work can help you get ahead.

1. Being published shows agents that you can manage submission deadlines and guidelines and that you are a serious writer with serious goals. You establish yourself as savvy and in touch by being published in smaller markets.

2. If editors are publishing your short works, it means they believe their readers will enjoy your writing. When an agent sees that other people are getting excited about your writing, he or she will be more likely to want in on the action.

3. Having credentials in the small press market may help you stand out from the competition. Most agents are aware of how difficult it is to secure one single publishing credit. It may be enough to sway an agent into representing you. If an agent is offered two books of equal merit—with the only difference being that one author has a history of publishing short works and the other doesn't—you can guess which book will get the contract.

4. Not only will publishing your shorter works make you a more interesting prospect, but having those publications is emotionally rewarding. Acceptance letters from literary magazines go a long way toward keeping you motivated as you write your book. A short story can be written in less than a week, whereas a book can take years. Keep your dream alive with smaller publications of short works.

5. Publishing in literary magazines might directly help you with getting an agent. A number of our clients have been approached by literary agencies because an agent read a story in a literary magazine. Getting your work, your name, and your bio out there can get you noticed in much the same way a model might get noticed simply by hanging around at the hottest nightclubs. Add a blurb to your bio that you are "currently working on a novel," and those who have enjoyed your work can be on the lookout for future projects.

6. More and more, literary agents are looking for clients who already have a built-in author platform. (An author platform is essentially the author's preexisting public reach via social media and traditional media.) Having a few publication credits before you submit your book to literary agents suggests that you are primed to make new fans.

But—remember this: You do not necessarily *need* to have publication credits in order to get a literary agent or to connect with a major publisher. Some authors have become best sellers without having had a single prior publishing credit to their name. Just know that it might be *easier* if you do have publication credits.

If you do not have any publication credits, and you do not have the time to dedicate to building an impressive portfolio, here are a few things you can do:

Join a well-known writing organization. Are you writing romance? Join Romance Writers of America. Are you into high-end literary works? Check out the Association of Writing Programs. You will probably need to spend some money to join these organizations, but the benefits are endless. First, you'll get to put their well-known name on your cover or query letter. Second, you'll get access to lots of great resources and you'll score great networking opportunities. And third, you'll show the agent or editor of your dreams that you're committed to and serious about your writing—whether you've published anything or not.

Attend a writing workshop. Writers all over the country are conducting workshops, and they may be meeting in your area. By being able to include in your bio, "I attend a weekly writing workshop meeting," you show that you're resourceful and diligent. Not only that, but your writing technique will benefit greatly, and you may meet other like-minded writers and make friends! Often these types of meetings are free. You can find them by looking into various social-networking sites online; just be sure to take all necessary precautions to stay safe.

Volunteer. By volunteering for the spring cleanup at your local library— or by devoting your time to other worthy endeavors—you demonstrate that you care deeply about literacy. Editors and agents like to see writers who truly have hearts of gold!

Take classes. Even if you don't have many (or any) publishing credentials, taking a class online or at your local community college establishes your dedication to being a professional writer. It will help your technique and your reputation. Editors and agents like to see writers who are actively committed to their craft. Being able to write, "I took a class at the University of XYZ" may strike a chord with agents and editors, since they are familiar with many writing programs. If you can't get to a school, check out online classes.

Go to a writing conference. If your budget permits, attend a writing conference. Not only will you learn and network, but you'll also be able to mention that you attended said conference in your bio. A writing conference is like an awards show after-party—everyone who's anyone will be there. If an agent or editor recognizes the name of the conference (maybe he or she attended or, perhaps, knows a colleague who did), that may tip the scales in your favor.

Submission Strategy Step #2:
Know Your Book Genre Inside And Out

So many writers who come to Writer's Relief do not have an expert grasp of their own book genre. This is a major problem with many writers who are approaching literary agents. While there are plenty of novels that have been published that defy all conventions of genre, it's important to represent your book as accurately and specifically as possible. If you botch your genre and the corresponding word count, you'll have an uphill battle. Literary agents tend to prefer books that they can easily identify and see where they fit on a bookstore shelf.

There's a lot that we could say about every single book genre out there. For now, we're going to offer you some basic pointers. The most important thing you can do is read and read (and read some more!). Reading is the best way to acquire an intimate knowledge of your book genre. There's simply no substitute.

Most books fall into one of three categories: literary, mainstream/general fiction, or genre/commercial fiction. Before you send your query to a literary agent, it's important to know what you're writing.

What Is Literary Fiction? How Do You Know If Your Book Qualifies As Literary?

Literary fiction is fiction of ideas. While the story must be good, emphasis on action is not as important as emphasis on the ideas, themes, and concerns of the book. Literary fiction tackles big issues that are often controversial, difficult, and complex.

Aside from subject matter, literary fiction tends to be written with emphasis on prose style. While genre fiction is "transparent" (readers can see through the text to escape into the story itself), literary writers want the reader to notice how beautiful the writing is. Sometimes the writing prevents the reader from escaping into the story, but that's not considered a negative in this genre.

Literary fiction is very specialized and difficult to do well. Literary readers (especially readers of experimental and "high literary" forms) are very demanding and are sometimes regarded as a niche market.

What Is General Fiction? How Do You Know If Your Book Qualifies As Mainstream?

Mainstream fiction, which goes by many other names (like general fiction and literary light), is driven by a mix of genre fiction and literary fiction techniques. In mainstream fiction, the writer must have a strong hook or premise. The story must be readable (it must have a traditional plot arc and be relatively plot- and character-driven). Controversy is welcome, but it is not presented in as nuanced a way as in literary fiction. Insight and emotionality are important, but the story is equally important.

Mainstream fiction tends to blend transparent language with occasional bouts of prose that feel more literary in tone. Writers of general fiction can have a variety of voices and write in a variety of styles, but all are accessible and not too difficult to read.

That said, keep in mind that the boundaries between the genres can be blurred. One person's literary novel might be another person's mainstream book.

How Long Is A Literary Novel? How Long Is A Mainstream Novel?

A literary novel can be between 40,000 and 120,000 words long. If you're a new writer, literary agents and editors will likely want to see a novel between 70,000 and 100,000 words. A mainstream novel is usually best suited when it hits the 70,000–100,000 mark as well.

Genre/Commercial Fiction

Genre fiction refers to books that are published widely for popular appeal. Usually, genre books are published in the smaller, mass-market book size.

Disclaimer: Please keep in mind that the information presented here is an overview of generalized genre guidelines: Always research information about your specific project for the best results. Also, remember that some authors have tackled "commercial" genres with huge "literary" success.

Romance Novels

A romance novel ends with a happily ever after. It starts with the introduction of characters and the conflict, and at some point the relationship is consummated in some way. The story usually emphasizes the heroine's experience, and the reader should be drawn into caring about the characters and cheering on the eventual romance.

A single-title (or stand-alone) romance novel runs between 80,000 and 100,000 words. A category romance novel (like those published by Harlequin) is generally shorter, and each "line" (or imprint) will have its own strict specifications. Save yourself a lot of trouble: Research before you write!

Subgenres of romance include paranormal, erotica, Regency, historical, contemporary, women's fiction, Christian, time travel, fantasy/science fiction, and more.

Women's Fiction

Women's fiction novels tend to be stories that focus on intense emotionality and relationships. Family members, friendships, the rigors of growing older, and the courage to pursue forgotten dreams are all fodder for women's fiction. Women's fiction can feature a romantic element, but the romance is not necessarily the element that drives the story.

Women's fiction novels tend to be between 80,000 and 100,000 words. At the time of this writing, women's fiction can be either historical or contemporary.

Fantasy Novels

Create the parameters of your fantasy world in advance and stick to them. Design the environment (geography, weather), the characters (race, creatures), and other details such as the use of magic, the history of your environment (wars, etc.), and limitations of powers.

How long are fantasy novels? Between 80,000 and 150,000 words (approximately). They can be a little longer than traditionally published novels and are sometimes serialized.

Subgenres of fantasy include alternate history, urban, dark, high, historical, steampunk, wuxia, fantasy of manners, and more.

Westerns

Westerns should be set in the Old West (west of the Mississippi River and before the year 1900). Historical details should be accurate.

Westerns tend to be on the shorter side of fiction books: anywhere from 45,000 to 75,000 words (loosely).

Historical Fiction

The details are important in this genre. Set the stage carefully and accurately so that your 18th-century character doesn't wear clothing or use products or idioms that weren't around at the time. We recommend conducting research on your chosen details prior to querying agents.

Generally, a stand-alone historical novel may be 85,000 to 100,000 words. For first-time writers, submitting a book longer than 100,000 words is especially difficult, but historical novels have been known to be on the long side. Historicals can fall anywhere on the spectrum of literary fiction, mainstream fiction, and genre fiction.

Mystery Novels

Create a solvable puzzle for your readers—mystery novels are supposed to be fun to read and fun to solve, but if the reader isn't provided with plausible clues to follow, they'll lose interest.

Mysteries vary in length depending on subgenre. Single-title mysteries may be between 75,000 and 100,000 words. Cozy mysteries, like those in a mystery series, may be on the shorter side.

Subgenres of mystery include hardboiled, supernatural, crime, true crime, amateur sleuth, police procedural, cozy, and more. Know the difference between a mystery and a thriller—and know which one you're writing.

Thrillers

Thrillers are designed to do one thing: thrill. Strong characters, tight plots, and an emphasis on action over flowery prose drive this genre to daring storylines. Thrillers often feature determined protagonists and clear antagonists, and they can be set in almost any location imaginable. Thrillers can be graphic (gritty) or somewhat more subtle, but the focus is always on suspense. Thrillers often incorporate a mystery element, but perhaps without the intellectually driven "puzzle book" sensibility that is often associated with mysteries.

Thriller novels hit the genre-standard sweet spot of 90,000 to 100,000 words for new writers. Thrillers tend to go a little longer as well, but new writers will probably see better results with shorter books.

Subgenres of thrillers include action, conspiracy, disaster, crime, eco, political, erotic, psychological, legal, and more.

Horror

Horror novels capitalize on fears and phobias. Create a feeling of dread for your reader, and sustain the suspense throughout until you reach a climactic conclusion.

Horror novels vary in length, but generally, a stand-alone novel will be between 80,000 and 100,000 words.

Subgenres of horror include psychological, ghost, weird menace, erotic, body horror, occult detective, and more.

Science Fiction

Science fiction blends science and technology, pushing our imaginations to the limit but still featuring elements of reality. Sci-fi novels tend to explore alternative possibilities and are often filled with thoughtful commentary.

Science fiction novels can vary in length, but generally speaking, a stand-alone sci-fi novel may run between 90,000 and 120,000 words.

Subgenres include hard, soft, cyberpunk, space western, alternate history, space opera, military, and more.

Young Adult (YA)

Young adult (YA) fiction targets readers between the ages of 12–18. The tone, style, and content of YA novels can vary significantly, depending on the specific age a writer is targeting. YA writers write for a specific audience without talking down.

Young adult novels vary in length based on the demographic, but generally run between 40,000 and 100,000 words or more, depending on the targeted age group.

Subgenres of YA include most of the same subgenres of adult fiction. Edgy YA tackles especially controversial or difficult issues.

New Adult

New adult is a relatively new genre that features protagonists in their twenties who are transitioning from young adulthood to full adulthood. New adult fiction can often be more explicit than young adult fiction in terms of violence and sex.

New adult fiction can range anywhere from 80,000 to 100,000 words.

Still Don't Know Your Book Genre?

Sometimes a writer simply doesn't know what genre his or her book fits into. And while it certainly can help your cause if your book fits neatly into a single genre, don't lose hope if your book's category isn't so cut and dried.

The Dangers Of Overly Obscure Book Genres

The number of book genres and subgenres out there is dizzying (especially for novels!). There are so many genres, we wager that even literary agents and editors have a hard time keeping them straight. For certain books, pigeonholing a project into a genre that's too narrow or obscure might suggest to literary agents that there isn't a big market for it (if they haven't heard of the genre, they might assume nobody else has either).

The Dangers Of Overly Broad Book Genres

If you write in your query letter: *Please consider my 100,000-word adventure, sci-fi romance with a touch of steampunk that may be suitable for young adults and adults because it appeals to everyone,* then an agent or editor might think, *How on earth can I market this book successfully?* There's no niche.

Rather than boasting, *Everyone will love this book,* decide, *Who is the best reader for my particular kind of novel? If I were in a bookstore, which shelf would this be found on?*

That's your genre.

What To Do If Your Genre Is Mixed

Sometimes, the line between book genres can be thin. For example: A women's fiction novel may have as its centerpiece a strong romantic story. Is it romance? Is it women's fiction?

If you think your book genre is romance and a potential agent thinks it is women's fiction, there may be some unwanted friction or misunderstandings (especially if the agent thinks the book genre label you chose doesn't fit your book!).

When you're pitching a book and you're not totally certain of the genre, it may be best to simply omit the specific genre from your letter and leave it to the agent to decide. Or you could mention that the book might be positioned, carefully and deliberately, within more than one genre.

What matters is that agents like the book—regardless of genre. If they like it, they'll help you figure out the best place to position it. Just be sure that the blurb (or mini-synopsis) in your query letter is strong enough to give them a clear idea of the direction of your book.

To some extent, the genre of your book can depend less on what's between the pages and more on what a publisher decides to do for marketing and positioning. However, the fact that your book genre is ultimately up to your publisher is no excuse to be uneducated about genre if you're trying to make a career as a writer. You should be familiar with the nuances of your favorite genres through reading. Don't write off genre entirely, but don't stress too much about it either. Focus on reading books that will help you write good books. That's what matters.

Do you feel like you've adequately prepared yourself to query literary agents?

Have you arranged your author bio as best you can?

Have you identified where your book fits in the larger marketplace?

Then it's time to start writing your query letter!

Submission Strategy Step #3:
Write A Strong Query Letter

As we stated in our introduction, there are many books out there about how to write a query letter (your one-page pitch to an agent). If you'd like to know more about advanced strategies for query letter writing, we hope you'll visit the Writer's Relief website and check out our books and articles about query writing techniques.

In this book, we're going to focus on the bigger picture. In other words, this book will tackle what so many other books do not: not just the writing of the query letter, but all the elements that come together to make a query letter possible.

Just so we're on the same page, let's take a quick look at what a query letter is.

QUERY LETTER: A one-page letter addressed to a literary agent that describes the key elements of your book and provides your biography so that the agent can decide if he or she would like to see more of the manuscript.

The Main Parts Of The Query Letter

When you send out a query letter to a literary agent, you have to know what to include. There are four necessary parts to a query letter, and it's up to you to decide the best order to place them in. Writers with impressive backgrounds, publishing credits, or expertise in their subject matter may choose to highlight their credentials at the beginning. An unpublished writer may choose to wow the editor by starting with the premise of the story.

The important thing is to cover all the fundamentals:

1) The Genre And Word Count

Many writers are tempted to start their query letters with a snazzy attempt at humor, a rhetorical question, or some witticism. Unfortunately, if the first line of a query letter is too flashy or splashy, it will often fall flat. Better to take a moderate and professional tone.

We recommend starting with the basic facts about your book. An agent will likely make the decision to read further based on the book genre and marketable word count alone. Make it clear what you are offering, and define your work in terms of genre and length.

Examples:

I hope you'll enjoy my 90,000-word women's fiction novel, Blue Sunday, *which was inspired by a family member who struggled with bulimia.*

Please consider my 110,000-word science fiction novel, The Grass Grows On Jupiter.

2) Blurb (or Overview)

Describe the plot of your story (or the concept of your nonfiction book). Keep it to less than 200 words if possible, and give just enough information to describe the general plot, the setting, central characters, and the conflict. You shouldn't give away the ending—better to leave your reader wanting more. Visit bookstores or libraries and study the back-cover summaries of books in your genre.

3) Your Credentials

Composing your professional writing bio is an easy task for previously published authors and experts, but may seem daunting to the unpublished writer. Whether you've got a string of best sellers behind you or this is your first writing endeavor, make sure you come across as confident (but not arrogant). If your query letter is good, your lack of experience need not count against you.

Highlight any publishing credentials, writing experience, and education. Know the best way to highlight self-published books in your bio.

Examples:

I've published numerous short stories in Literary Magazine *and have a degree in journalism from Impressive College.*

This book is based on my findings while on an archaeological dig in Africa for Snooty University, where I currently teach archaeology.

If your background experience has no bearing on the subject, leave it out. However, if your writing credentials are not impressive, by all means highlight anything in your background that merits writing your book. Example:

As a mother of a child with Down syndrome, I feel uniquely qualified to write about the subject.

4) Thank You

In closing, be sure to thank the editor or agent for his or her time and offer to send sample chapters (if not already included) or the complete manuscript. Enclose a self-addressed, stamped envelope for convenience if you are querying by mail.

What Else?

These four elements provide the basic structure for your query letter. Within this framework there's actually quite a lot of technique and strategy involved. Working with writers since 1994, we have found that qualities that make a person a good novelist or memoirist do not necessarily make that person a good query letter writer. Query letter writing requires a much different kind of skill than book writing. So if you struggle with writing your query letter, don't worry. You're not alone.

How To Find Out More About Writing A Killer Query

The good news is that we offer query letter writing tips on our website that contain advanced strategies to help your letter stand out among the hundreds of letters that literary agencies receive each month. Years of experience have shown us what works and what does not work. We hope you will visit our website and check it out.

However, if you would rather work with an experienced professional to create your query letter, you are welcome to contact Writer's Relief with your inquiry. Our professional query letter writers can help you create a letter that will present your book at its very best. You only get one shot at querying an agent with your letter, so make it a great one!

Many writers have managed to get a literary agent without professional assistance from Writer's Relief or any other aid. You *can* become a good query letter writer on your own, as long as you're prepared to put in the time and effort to learn the etiquette and strategies. Don't shrug off the importance of a skillfully prepared query letter. And don't make the mistake of thinking that being able to write a book automatically means you can write a fantastic query. A little research on your part will go a long way.

Here are some additional ways to learn the more advanced techniques of query letter writing:

- Go to the library and find a book on query writing
- Connect with your local writing group and attend a workshop about query letter writing
- Go to a writing conference and participate in a seminar about how to write a query letter

Once your query letter is ready, you can move on to the next piece of your "perfect pitch": your synopsis!

Submission Strategy Step #4:
Tackle The Tough Job Of Writing Your Synopsis

These days, few literary agents ask for a synopsis when you send your query: They will request your synopsis only if they like your query letter. That said, you need to have your synopsis ready before you start sending out your queries so that you can respond quickly if you receive requests.

Writers often hate the job of writing a book synopsis. As anxiety escalates, so many questions rush through their minds: *What is a literary agent looking for in my synopsis or summary? How many details should I include? Should I explain my setting and characters or just stick to the basic plot?*

For now, let's start with the fundamentals.

What is a synopsis for a book or novel?

A synopsis for a novel is different than a book blurb for a novel. A book blurb is a short description of your novel in a query letter. A synopsis is a longer, more complete description of the entire story. A synopsis may accompany your query letter or be sent later if the agent requests additional information about your book.

Generally speaking, a full-length synopsis is usually requested from writers who are working in the genre of fiction or memoir. Prescriptive nonfiction writers (like self-help and how-to) do not necessarily have to submit a traditional synopsis.

If you are writing prescriptive nonfiction, we recommend that you just skim the next two sections in this topic. We'll address how nonfiction manuscripts are pitched to literary agents in the "Special Considerations" section.

1. How should you format the pages of your synopsis? Write your synopsis in the same format as your manuscript. Double-space your synopsis. Use one-inch margins all around. Do NOT full-justify your text. Use left justification only. Put a header on every page. Use 12-point Times New Roman or Arial font. Do not use Courier font.

2. How should you begin your synopsis? Begin by broadly describing your story in 25 words or less, if possible. You must capture the agent's attention.

3. What verb tense should you use for your synopsis? Include a COMPLETE summary of your story from beginning to end, written in present tense. Focus on major plot points or turning points. Omit secondary characters, subplots, and minor events. Don't go into too much detail.

4. What should you focus on in your synopsis? Include the setting, main characters, and the all-important CONFLICT. Then, show the resolution of this conflict.

5. Should you tell the ending of your book in your synopsis? Yes, you should. We know you want to keep readers guessing, but the novel synopsis is not the place for it. Leave the teasing for the book blurb in your query letter!

6. Should you ask rhetorical questions in your synopsis to keep readers interested? Do not ask empty questions in your synopsis. Doing so will not fool the agent into asking for the remaining pages of your manuscript.

7. Does proofreading really matter in your synopsis? Yes, absolutely. Proofread your synopsis. Make sure grammar, punctuation, and spelling are perfect.

8. Should you write your synopsis in first person from a character's perspective or third person? Write your synopsis in third person for a novel. If you are writing a memoir, use first person.

9. How long is a synopsis for a novel? There are no industry-wide rules at this point to dictate the length of your synopsis. Each agent will have a different preference.

Our advice: If you're going to write only one synopsis, limit it to just one or two pages (three at most). In our experience, it's better to come in under the requested page count than over.

Submission Strategy Step #5:
Prepare Your Opening Pages

Should a literary agent or editor be interested in your novel or memoir after reading your query letter and/or your synopsis, then you need to ensure that your opening pages are equally engaging.

The first five pages are extremely important if you want to capture a literary agent's attention. If a book's opening pages are not compelling, the chances of successfully connecting with a literary agency are drastically reduced.

Excuses, Excuses

Although most writers know that their opening pages need to be stellar, newer writers frequently have trouble getting themselves to not only *know* that fact, but to *accept* it and do something about it.

Some writers push themselves and do whatever's necessary to write a compelling opening—even to the point of rewriting the entire book. But other writers tend to be less critical of their own technique. "If only the literary agent would read the second chapter," they say. "That's when the book gets interesting."

In theory, there's nothing wrong with asking an agent to read all the way through the second chapter to get involved in a great book. But the fact is, almost *no* literary agents will do that. Neither will readers.

Consider this: If you have twenty dollars to buy one of two equally good books—the only difference being that one has a great beginning and the other one doesn't—which would you purchase?

If you find yourself making excuses for your opening pages, it may be time to face the truth: The better your opening, the better your shot at getting an agent.

Novels: Two Common Opening Turnoffs

There are a number of opening gambits that writers would be wise to avoid. Here are two that we see frequently:

Unnecessary prologues. Most prologues do little to grab a reader's attention—they're big and splashy but often lack substance and are inappropriate for the tone of the book. Sometimes they can be effective hooks—only for chapter one to fall back on dull, old techniques. If you're determined to use a prologue, make sure it's totally necessary and consistent with the tone of the rest of your book. If you can leave it out, we highly recommend you do so.

Backstory. Some books are bogged down with recalling everything that happened to set up the story before getting to the actual story. As a result, the plotline doesn't get interesting until a hundred or so pages into the book. And the reader often gives up long before reaching that point. Writers sometimes find it difficult to understand where their narrative begins, and spend too much time describing things that happened in the past. But the power of a story lies in how it looks forward, not back.

For example: A writer is composing a story about a cop whose unusual approach to solving crime stems from his experiences a few years ago when his own home was burglarized. A new writer—thinking linearly—might be inclined to begin the narrative at the beginning, starting with the cop's house being robbed and showing his evolution toward his particular kind of crime fighting. But a veteran writer would start in the present—a cop fighting crime in an unusual way—and then weave in the backstory as needed.

Here are four tips to keep in mind for the first five pages of your novel or memoir:

1. Opening Action

Your opening pages must grab or hook the reader. One of the best ways to do that is to start with an intense and important moment. It doesn't have to be a momentous save-the-world crisis; it might be something as small as a fifth grader trying to figure out where to sit in the cafeteria.

What's essential is that you invest the moment with gravity and consequence. The character might be on the brink of real change or perhaps facing a decision that will affect the people in his or her life. Whatever you open with, make it clear that it's important—vitally important—to the entire plot to come.

2. Characters

Of course, whatever character you choose to focus on should be fascinating. Show the reader right away why it's worth spending time with your character. Is she courageous and selfless? Excellent! Readers want to spend time with heroes and heroines they admire. Is he devious, sinister, and complex? Perfect! We love villains who are multidimensional, who believe they're doing right—or who can't stop themselves from doing wrong.

Your characters must draw your audience in. Show the reader what your characters want, and present a scene in which they are trying to get it.

NOTE: Be careful that you don't introduce too many characters at once. Hook your reader with ONE character first, and don't introduce other characters until you're sure that you've set the hook in deep.

3. Setting

Choosing a fabulous, unique, larger-than-life, out-of-the-ordinary setting for your opening pages will offer a higher interest factor. Rendering your setting in surprising and distinct detail will draw the reader into your world. Open your book somewhere your readers have never been, and you'll lure them in.

BUT—if your opening isn't set in Antarctica or the forgotten storeroom of a traveling Believe-It-Or-Not show, don't fret. What's important is to present your setting in a way that will make something about it surprising or new to your readers. You may have an opening scene in a familiar landscape—say, the cafeteria again—but it's how you render the scene that can make it amazing and fascinating. Use the POV (point of view) of your character to offer details that the reader may have taken for granted, details that are quietly amazing.

4. Momentum

Perhaps what's most crucial about your first scene is its momentum—the force that leads readers into the next page, and the next, and the next. Your opening pages should NOT be answering questions about your characters' quest or your characters' past. The opening should be asking them.

Think of your opening pages as the open door to your book. Your task is to invite and intrigue the reader and get them to come inside—and you can't do that without creating a sense of anticipation. So don't offer everything you've got in your first pages. Tempt the reader to read on.

Special Considerations: Prescriptive Nonfiction Books

If you are writing something other than a novel or a memoir, this next section is for you.

Novels and memoirs are traditionally handled the same way: The writer creates a query letter with a short synopsis in order to pitch a *completed* book.

Nonfiction books, such as self-help and how-to books, do not have to be completed prior to submission to literary agents and editors; nonfiction is sold to editors via book proposal. It's important to know what to include in a nonfiction book proposal.

In general, the nonfiction book proposal is designed to give editors a well-organized, detailed sales pitch describing what your proposed book is about and how it will make money for the publishing company.

An additional bonus is that writing a book proposal forces the author to organize and focus the project. The book itself may go through many changes depending on editorial input, but the proposal should follow a generally accepted format.

NOTE: Even though a memoir is a nonfiction book, you don't need to write a proposal for your true story. Literary agents do not want to read a proposal for memoir. A memoir is usually handled the same way as a novel: The book must be complete, and the writer must submit sample chapters.

If you are writing a proposal for your nonfiction book, you should familiarize yourself with the advanced techniques used to create a strong proposal. For now, let's start with the basics.

Components Of A Proposal:

Title Page

In your nonfiction proposal you should include your name, contact information, approximate word count, and the proposed title of your book. Make sure your main title describes the subject matter of the book so that readers can find it easily in Internet keyword searches. Don't rely on subtitles to convey vital information—subtitles are often dropped in computerized listings and library databases. Note: The title you choose is your working title; publishers may elect to change it.

**Optional: Summary (aka Overview, Synopsis, or Executive Summary) – 1-page maximum

Begin with a very short description of your book's basic premise. Whatever makes your book stand out should be highlighted in the first few sentences. This is the hook, so make it interesting and unique, powerful yet concise.

Capture the editor's attention immediately, and make it clear what you're selling. If the literary agent or editor has to hunt around for the point of your book, he or she is likely to toss your proposal aside and move on to the next proposal in the towering slush pile.

Chapter By Chapter Outline – 1 to 2 paragraphs per chapter

Create a dynamic outline by highlighting each chapter's major points. Each chapter synopsis should be no longer than one or two paragraphs— you don't want to give too much information, but you don't want to give too little either.

Emphasize each chapter's unique and/or important function(s) in relation to the rest of the book. By the time the agent/editor has finished reading your outline, he or she should have a clear idea of the overall book.

The Market For Your Nonfiction Book

This section should include information about the book's intended market and why your book effectively addresses the needs of that particular audience. Make sure that your market is broad (as in "women ages 30–60" or "people who buy cars"), and provide as many demographics of your targeted audience as possible. Include observations about current trends that favor your book and highlight what makes your book unique.

Also include information about the competition. If there are other books out there on the same subject, yours must offer a new or original take. Identify current books that are similar, and explain how yours fills a specific untapped niche. If there are complementary books out there, show how your book can be positioned to the publisher's advantage.

If possible, consider including endorsements from other writers who are expert in your field. Or, connect with an expert who is willing to create the introduction for your book and state that if the book finds a publisher, "so-and-so big-name author" has already agreed to write the introduction.

Give the literary agency enough ammunition to sell your work!

Author Information In A Nonfiction Book Proposal

This is where you list your education, writing credentials, contacts, experience—anything that makes you singularly qualified to write this book. If you don't have a degree directly related to your subject matter or a list of publishing credits, highlight any information that shows you have what it takes to tackle the subject.

For instance, you may be a parent of a special-needs child, and, although you have never been published, your experience qualifies you to offer an insider's perspective on how to successfully navigate through healthcare and educational red tape—assuming that your writing is up to par. If you have an author website, consider mentioning it here.

Your background (including your publishing credits, your experience and expertise, your media coverage, and the following of readers that you've built up) is often referred to as your platform. The stronger your platform, the better!

You should also outline your own promotional ideas and resources to help market the book. Include any affiliations, contacts, or endorsements you may have lined up. Do you have a prominent person willing to write the foreword? Media contacts? Websites, bookstore appearances, newsletters, and possible sequels or spin-off information should be included in this section. To use the example above, you may be a member of the Autism Society of America, and with the contacts you have made within that organization, you can offer greater promotional opportunities.

Specifications Of Your Unfinished Book

This is where you outline an approximate word count, the number of chapters, and an estimated time frame for completing your book. If your book will contain a number of charts, photographs, or illustrations, say so. You may also describe the general format you envision. However, be prepared to be flexible when it comes to length and format—the publisher will have the final say.

Note: A full-length nonfiction book is usually comprised of 9 to 15 chapters of average length, and between 80,000 and 100,000 words. Make sure you have enough material (and time) to fulfill this obligation before you propose it.

Table Of Contents

Quite simply, this is a list of chapter titles to give the agent or editor an idea of what will be included in your book.

Sample Chapters

If you have already begun the writing process, send one or two completed chapters (chapters 1 and 2 are preferable).

Other Tips:

Your book proposal should be similar in style to your proposed book. In other words, if your book is meant to be humorous and lighthearted, make sure your proposal is written in the same style.

Make sure the proposal is thoroughly—thoroughly!—edited and proof-read. Literary agents admit to passing over potentially great ideas if they have to wade through a sea of errors, typos, and coffee stains.

Always include a self-addressed stamped envelope (SASE) for responses if you are submitting by mail. The proposal you send will be recycled, not returned. If you're submitting online, be sure you know the etiquette and requirements.

When formatting, we recommend using a 12-point, easy-to-read font like Times New Roman or Arial, with one-inch margins all around, and left justification. But, as always, defer to each agent's submission guidelines when available.

Special Considerations: Short Story Collections

We're approached by countless writers every year who want help submitting their short story collections to literary agents. The short story is an exciting literary form that many writers have mastered, but few writers truly understand how to get a collection of short stories published.

It takes talent and practice to make short stories work. Some novelists begin their careers with stories and work their way up to longer forms (novels or memoirs). Other writers prefer to work in the short form and eventually find themselves with a stack of stories several inches high, wondering, "Why not turn my short stories into a collection?"

Short stories are becoming increasingly popular, not only because they are mini works of art, but also because busy people have shorter attention spans. There are hundreds of literary magazines and journals that publish individual stories (and Writer's Relief keeps tabs on all of them), but finding a home for a collection of short stories is no easy task.

Major publishers want novels because they sell, and they rarely consider novellas or collections of short stories. Short story collections are harder to place because editors are often reluctant to take chances on unknown writers.

Before you protest about the number of successful anthologies on the market, be aware that anthologies are generally collections of stories by a number of different authors—collections appealing to readers who are looking for a particular theme or subject matter. Anthologies of work by a single, unknown author tend to be difficult to sell.

Many writers get frustrated and end up self-publishing their short story collections, especially if they're simply looking for limited quantities to give to family and friends.

Even though the odds may not be in your favor, don't let us completely discourage you from trying to get your short story collection published—there are some things you can do to increase your chances.

Publish selected works. It's easier to sell a collection if you've had at least a few short stories previously published in reputable literary journals. Submit individual stories to quality magazines on a regular basis, and with each publication credit, your credibility will increase.

At Writer's Relief we highly recommend that writers build their credits first rather than approach literary agents with a group of unpublished stories. National exposure in quality magazines is key to attracting an agent's attention.

Have a theme. It helps if the stories have a common theme or subject to tie them together. James Herriot was a country vet, not an aspiring author, but his collection of stories had a cohesive theme, and the *All Creatures Great and Small* series is still popular today.

Make it a novel. Some agents recommend scrapping the whole idea of a collection and refashioning it into a novel or even a "novel-in-stories." They might also suggest selling the collection as part of a two-book deal, with the story collection designed to generate interest in the second book, which would be an actual novel (or vice versa).

Enter as many short story writing competitions as possible. An award-winning story can land a publishing deal. It can also boost a writer's self-confidence—always a bonus!

Consider small presses. There are far more small presses than big publishing houses, and they often specialize in niche markets. They also tend to publish out of love for the genre and may be more receptive to a short story collection if they admire the quality of your work.

Get a literary agent. If you have an agent, your chances of selling a collection are better than for unagented writers. To get an agent for a short story collection, you'll need a strong bio. It may also help to mention in your query letter that you have a novel in the works, if that is the case.

Get educated. Short story collections are far easier to sell when their authors have top-notch credentials: publication credits in quality magazines, awards, grants, etc. Graduating from a quality MFA program is a plus as well.

Special Considerations: Essay Collections

There is a market for individually published personal essays—themed anthologies, newspapers, literary magazines, trade and professional journals—but selling a compilation of essays takes extra marketing savvy.

The means of generating interest in an essay collection are similar to those available to short story writers. Here are some strategies for garnering interest in an essay collection.

Publication credits. If you've previously published essays in reputable literary journals, make sure to include these credits in your query letter. We highly recommend that you build your publication credits before approaching an agent with a collection of unpublished essays. The market for an essay collection is limited unless you have significantly newsworthy experiences or have a background that proves your writing has mass appeal. Numerous publication credits will indicate readers' interest in your work.

Theme. Collections do well when they include essays with a common theme. For example, David Sedaris is best known for his humorous essays, and C. S. Lewis once published a collection of religious essays. Examples of other themes include women's studies, travel, sports, or city life. Unique themes get attention—people love to read about real-life experiences that are highly unusual—but even the most outrageous stories must be backed by good writing.

Your author platform. With creative nonfiction, you're selling your personality and your experiences. If you have any notoriety, you'll find it easier to publish your essay collection. But if not, don't worry! It's the strength of your story that counts most.

Is your pitch perfect?

Do you know your book project inside and out?

Have you determined how your book fits in the larger market?

How will you "sell" it to publishing professionals?

Then let's take the next step!

Part Three

The Submission Process

Identify And Entice The Right Literary Agent
For Your Book

When Does Your Relationship With Your Future Agent Really Start?

Believe it or not, your relationship with your future literary agent starts even before you think of writing your query letter. It begins the moment you start thinking about what kind of literary agent you want to have.

Now that you know how to position your book within the larger marketplace and how to present yourself as "the complete package," let's take the next step. It's time to understand what you're looking for (and what you're not) in your future agent.

Self-Test: What Kind Of Literary Agent Is Right For You?

Every literary agent has his or her own style—just like you! So if you are looking for a literary agent, how do you know what kind of agent is best for you?

It's important to know what you want. If you have an idea of what you're looking for *before* you start looking, you and your future literary agent are more likely to find that your partnership brings a lot of success.

Use These Questions To Determine The Kind Of Literary Agent That Will Work Best For You

1. How do you like to communicate? Some literary agents use email exclusively. Others prefer phone calls from clients. There are literary agents willing to meet face-to-face with their clients (or their potential clients), but also those who do not prioritize one-on-one meetings.

So, how do you want to communicate? If your initial conversations with your potential agent do not give you a clear indication of communication preferences, then just ask.

2. How much critique do you want or need? Most literary agents offer some level of critique for a new client. But do you want a literary agent to be critiquing your writing? Or do you feel that the editorial process should happen exclusively between writer and editor? Know what you want so that you can ask the right questions when you begin talking to your potential agent.

3. Do you want an experienced agent? Or a brand-new agent? What established literary agents might offer in the way of experience, new literary agents could counter with lots of enthusiasm and drive. We will elaborate on this in an upcoming section.

4. Are you willing to work with a literary agent who has only just begun to represent books in your genre? Some literary agents decide, mid-career, that they want to work with a different genre. For example: An agent who has typically represented nonfiction might decide one day that he or she wants to take on a few novels. Are you open to working with a literary agent who has experience and enthusiasm—but perhaps not the personal, established connections with editors within your genre?

5. Which is better: a big literary agency or small agent who works alone? When you're deciding which type of literary agent will work best for your writing goals, one of the first things you should determine is whether or not you want to work with a big, well-known literary agency or with an independent literary agent.

Let's examine the pros and cons of large and small agencies. Then you can make your decision about which literary agents to query.

The Benefits Of Boutique Or Independent Literary Agents

While large literary agencies might host dozens of literary agents under the same company umbrella, a boutique literary agency is often just one or two literary agents doing the bulk of the job.

Here are some of the many positives of a boutique or independent literary agent:

- With a less demanding client list, an independent literary agent might have more time to devote to you and your book.
- Even if your independent literary agent is not able to sell your first manuscript, he or she still might be willing to stick with you because of the personal connection you've established.
- An independent literary agent can offer many of the same services that a large literary agency provides, including subsidiary rights negotiations (like translation rights) and critique.
- If your boutique literary agency does not have a large number of high-profile clients, you may find yourself and your work being prioritized.

The Positive Side Of Large Literary Agencies

- Many literary agents working under the umbrella of one company means these agents can share their connections in order to make deals.
- Larger agencies often offer amenities such as: a foreign rights department, a speaker's bureau, partner agencies in other industries (such as film and TV), a lawyer on staff to review contracts, etc.
- Because they often represent best-selling authors and have a track record of success, big literary agencies can be powerful allies when it comes to contract negotiations.

The Drawbacks Of A Boutique Literary Agency

- A smaller agency may or may not have the "power" of a name behind it.
- If an agent is handling ALL subsidiary rights on his or her own, then he or she might not be able to focus on your subsidiary rights sales.
- The agent may or may not have the same kinds of connections as a multimember literary agency.
- A boutique literary agent can be just as overworked as a literary agent at a large company, depending on the number of clients the agent represents.

The Drawbacks Of A Large Literary Agency

- There is some danger that you might get "lost" in the large number of clients or the number of departments (if more than one person handles your work).
- A large agency may have separate departments dedicated to foreign rights and movie deals, but if you are not a big-name author, *you* might not be prioritized in those departments.
- An agent from a bigger agency could be more inclined to part ways with you if you are not making a profit. Or, you might simply be ignored.

A Caveat About Choosing The Size Of Your Literary Agency

The guidelines we have provided offer a general overview. There are no rules that can be applied to every single literary agent, whether they are at a boutique literary agency or a large company.

In other words, there are boutique literary agents who are working independently and negotiate phenomenal book deals on behalf of their clients. And there are literary agents who are part of "mega agencies" who may not be making very significant deals at all. And an independent literary agent could be just as likely as any large literary agency to drop you if you're not pulling your weight.

Whether you choose an independent agent working from home or a literary agent who is part of a centrally located larger group, there is one key attitude that you must look for in the literary agent who is going to represent your writing: enthusiasm, enthusiasm, enthusiasm. Unless a literary agent has a passion for your writing, it is unlikely that you will see your book succeed.

How To Spot A Bad Literary Agent

New novelists and veteran authors can fall prey to literary agency schemes—hidden tricks that unscrupulous literary agents use to fake legitimacy or make fast money. Writers should be wary.

A reputable literary agent should make money by selling books. That's it. If an agent is asking for any fees (reading, evaluations, marketing, or retainer fees), let the red flags unfurl.

Reading fees at agencies weren't always a red flag, but because several agencies began abusing the system—charging fees without having any genuine interest in the material itself—the practice was abolished by the Association of Authors' Representatives (or AAR, the trade group for U.S. literary agents).

The same goes for evaluation fees. If an agency offers an evaluation of your manuscript, it should be free. Disreputable agencies will sometimes charge the writer for a "critique," which is generic, widely applicable, or performed by an underqualified staff member. The AAR frowns upon this practice and so should you.

Other dubious fees fall under the category of administration, marketing, or submission costs. A good agent will only charge the client for expenses that are above and beyond normal and reasonable expenses, such as long-distance phone calls and shipping costs. But these are usually deducted from the client's royalties and should not be up-front costs.

Watch out for agents who demand money up front, especially for vague reasons. If in doubt, request an itemized list of any charges—you should not be billed for every sheet of notepaper your agent uses.

Sometimes an agent is not dishonest, but merely inept. This is an agent who uses questionable methods to submit your work to editors—sending your work to editors who aren't looking for what you are trying to sell, bundling several queries into one package, using shotgun types of submission methods, and not doing his or her homework.

These agents quickly develop a bad reputation among editors, and their clients can expect their books to be ignored. Some writers feel that any agent is better than none at all, but this simply is not the case.

Reputable agents do not need to advertise in magazines or search for clients online, and they never send spam. If you are approached by an agent without ever having contacted them, beware. Dishonest agents often troll online writer forums or purchase subscription lists from writer magazines in an attempt to beef up their client list.

NOTE: Once in a great while, an agent will read your work in a magazine and contact you directly; this is a legitimate practice, and you should be able to tell that it is not a generic form letter, that the agent actually read your work and admired it.

What steps can you take to avoid bad literary agencies?

Query only established agents. Seek a literary agent whose primary job is agenting (as opposed to writing or working in marketing). Some agents do write and agent, but it's important that agenting is his or her first priority. A good agent will wear one hat and one hat only.

Check track record/sales. The number-one indication of a successful agent will be his or her track record, and the agent should be eager to share this with you. If an agent claims recent sales are confidential, this is a red flag. Feel free to ask for recent sales, published works, recommendations from satisfied clients, etc.

Look for professionalism across the board. Is the agency's website or correspondence with you full of typos and/or grammatical errors? Does the agent get defensive or angry when you ask questions about fees and contract issues? Are your calls ignored for weeks? In general, look for professionalism and general courtesy from an agent.

Watch for "recommended services." If your agent gives your work high praise...and then suggests that it will only sell if it is professionally edited, you should immediately go on high alert, especially if the agent already has an editor for you (that you will have to pay for). This is usually the sign of a kickback referral scheme that preys on the hopes and dreams of new writers, and it is highly unethical. The same goes for illustrators. A good agent knows that publishers prefer to do the matching of authors and illustrators, and they should not push you to hire one they recommend.

Beware of agents who are looking for poets and short story writers. Most legitimate agents do not make any money off poetry and short fiction—unless the writer is already very strongly established.

Think twice about agents who shower you with excessive flattery and praise. Or those who make grand promises. (Good agents don't make promises they can't keep.)

Keep an eye out for signs of incompetence. There are plenty of mediocre agents out there who engage in unprofessional practices such as using the client's own query letters, employing random submission strategies, and insisting the client pay for 8×10 photos, fancy binders, and marketing plans (all of which are unnecessary and off-putting to editors).

**The bottom line: If it sounds too good to be true,
it probably is.**

Should You Query A Brand-New Literary Agent?

When you begin researching literary agents online or meeting them in person, you may find yourself wondering if it is appropriate to query a literary agent who does not yet have a lot of experience.

At Writer's Relief we are often asked this question, and our answer is yes, absolutely! Target a wide variety of agents, from the big names to the lesser known—assuming, of course, they're appropriate for your work and are ethical and reputable. It's tough to land an agent, and by making well-targeted submissions and casting an appropriately wide net, you'll increase your chances.

If your work does happen to interest a literary agent who has only been in business a short while, remember that anyone can claim to be an agent—there is no license or competency testing required to set up shop.

So before you sign with a new literary agent, ask these questions:

1. What's the literary agent's background?

A literary agent who opened his or her doors a year ago may have previously worked with a major publishing house or another reputable literary agency, and should have the skills and contacts necessary to place your work. But an agent with no experience (or contacts) in the industry and a background in commercial sales or advertising probably doesn't have the expertise you're looking for.

And if the agent is simply a frustrated writer who set him- or herself up as an agency because of feeling ignored by "the establishment," that person is probably not your best bet.

2. Is the agent solo or part of a larger group?

If your potential, inexperienced agent works with three or four established agents, their combined experience and contacts will likely work to your advantage. Many new agents get a strong start because they work in reputable offices that offer plenty of editorial and professional support.

If your agent works alone, at home, you may want to ask some additional questions. Where did the decision to work independently from home come from? Also, how often does the agent get into the city to hobnob with publishing types (one agent we know of reportedly traveled 500 miles by train to New York once a week in order to hold all her necessary meetings before returning home; other agents rely primarily on phone calls but have occasional trips to New York for face-time lunches with editors).

NOTE: Some reputable solo agents who've been around awhile do work from home to keep overhead costs down (or just because they can). When making a decision about submitting, this should be a contributing factor but not a determining one.

3. What kind of client list does he or she have?

A brand-new agent isn't going to have a long list of big-name clients or commercial book sales, but you should ask about any recently published or sold books. If the client list is a litany of unpublished writers, or authors who did not publish with reputable publishing houses, be careful— you don't want to end up being another name on that list too.
And consider the bonuses: Newer reps are actively trying to build up their client lists, so they are more likely to sign new writers. They will also have more time to really focus on those writers and work closely with them to get their book projects ready to submit.

4. What's his or her experience in contract negotiations?

Newer agents may be less experienced in contract negotiations, and as newbies, they may not have the clout that can help get huge advances for their authors. But it's important that your agent is knowledgeable about publishing contract terminology and is able to protect your rights. Not all agents are lawyers or work with lawyers, so ask questions about practical experience.

Agents who do not have a history of dealing with contracts will sometimes partner with intellectual property rights lawyers to assist with fine-print negotiations. Larger agencies will often have lawyers on staff.

5. What's the enthusiasm level?

Does your potential agent have big plans and an enthusiasm for your work? Does he or she have a well-targeted list of publishers in mind for submitting your novel? Are your calls and emails promptly responded to or usually ignored?

Newer agents are often excited and willing to put in the work to create a successful track record; if your potential agent is lackluster, unfocused, or generally unenthusiastic about you and your book, the publishers the agent approaches will adopt this attitude as well.

That said, amateur agents may have all the enthusiasm and good intentions in the world, but if they have no publishing experience and have shoddy business practices, they could do you more harm than good.

New agents can be phenomenal partners. The trick is to do your research in advance before you sign a contract. Who knows? Maybe you as a new writer and your agent as a new agent will become big names in publishing together!

Literary Agents As Publishers: Important To Know

There's something new going on in the literary world these days: Some literary agencies are starting up their own publishing divisions. If a literary agent can't sell a client's book (or if a client's book goes out of print), a literary agent can help his or her client to keep the book on the market in some form by publishing it.

Sometimes an agent will partner with an existing digital press, subsidy publisher, or a self-publishing company. "Publishing a book" can mean anything from giving the book a page on the site of an Internet bookseller (and nothing more) to national distribution and marketing in physical bookstores.

Is it ethical for a literary agent to also be a publisher?

Some arguments FOR agents who publish:

- They help authors do what authors would want to do anyway.
- They help their clients make a little more money.
- Agents are intimately familiar with their clients' projects and, therefore, can be an important contributor to packaging, marketing, and distribution strategies.
- Literary agents have an insider's view of the publishing industry that a writer alone might not have.
- Books that would have gone out of print or would have never been published are accessible to the public.
- Any book publicity is better than no book publicity.
- Agents can use their public profiles to sell books.
- Having an agent's help (for the equivalent of self-publishing) is better than no help at all.

Some arguments AGAINST agents who publish:

- Agents should represent a writer. But when an agent is also a publisher, the agent and writer are on two different sides.
- An agent is supposed to protect a writer during a contract negotiation—but with the agent acting as the publisher, contract negotiations become a conflict of interests.
- In theory, a good agent—an agent who is serious about making a sale—shouldn't need to fall back on publishing their clients' books. That's what publishers are for.

- Agents who are also publishers make money from publishing their clients' work. This may detract from an agents' primary commitment to get their clients' work published with third-party publishers.
- If a writer is locked into a contract that names the agent as publisher in the event that the agent can't sell the book, the writer could end up settling for a less favorable publishing deal than if the author had simply self-published with a different company or independent press.
- Being a literary agent and being a publisher are two different professions. There's some overlap but, ultimately, being an agent OR being a publisher can be a full-time job. There's the danger that an agent who is publishing may be spreading himself or herself too thin, or overestimating his or her ability to do everything.
- It's a bit of a gray area when an agent who represents a work also holds the rights to it. Ethical (and financial) questions can arise.

What you should do:

Know what you're getting into. If your potential agent does assist with self-publishing, be sure that you can keep your own copyright(s) and that *you* hold on to all rights to publish your book (instead of licensing rights to your agency). Understand that allowing your agent to publish your book with his or her own publishing subsidiary will possibly hinder your ability to publish your book elsewhere.

If you don't want your agent to publish your book, be very clear about that up front. If you don't like a literary agent's policies, get a different agent.

But if you like the idea of having help with publishing an out-of-print book or a book that didn't find a home at a big publishing house, then just be sure that you take an active and attentive role in your book's publication with your literary agency-cum-publisher.

Where To Start Your Search For A Literary Agent

How do you begin to research literary agents who will want to represent your novel, memoir, or nonfiction book?

As you know from our introduction, this is not another book that contains listings of literary agencies. We are trying to offer you a bigger picture of the publishing industry. But we do want to say a few words about where specifically you can turn if you're looking for a literary agent.

Writer's Relief can do the literary agent research for you if you don't have the time or would rather be writing than sifting through market books. But if you're planning to find a literary agent on your own, that's okay too!

Let's recap: Here are the elements you will need to have in place before you begin querying a literary agent.

Step 1: Finish your novel or memoir (or your nonfiction book proposal). Be sure your manuscript is polished and perfected.

Step 2: Get your bearings in the publishing industry. Know your genre and get to know the market you're targeting, as well as the ins and outs of the publishing industry. The fact that you're reading this book is a good sign! You are already on your way.

Step 3: Write your query letter. Have fun with the process of writing a query letter to pitch your book. Remember, the goal of your query is to present your book in the best possible light. And do what you can to present yourself as a serious, up-and-coming writer in your author bio.

Step 4: Create a list of suitable agents. Based on your particular genre, you can narrow down the list of possible agents to those who represent similar work.

There are several ways to do this:

- **Trade journals and guides.** Research directories that list literary agencies and publishers, such as the most current edition of *Writer's Market* or *Literary Marketplace*. (Remember that these listings can be out of date, so verify contact information and agent interests before submitting.) Cross-check information for verification.

- **Browse.** Spend some time in bookstores to find books similar to your own; sometimes authors will mention their agents in the acknowledgments section. Read book reviews and interviews with authors who publish in your genre—they often mention their agents by name.

- **Networking.** Ask other authors who have published work in your genre for agent recommendations, and, if at all possible, get a referral that you can mention in your query letter. Attend writers conferences and workshops where you can meet agents and successful authors. Writers groups can also offer good networking opportunities.

- **Internet.** There's a wealth of information online, but the Internet can also be a breeding ground for disreputable agents and unfounded gossip within the writing community. Do your research in advance to check on an agent's background. We will show you how in a later section.

Step 5: Create a specific submission schedule and hold yourself to it. How many literary agents should you query before you give up? Here at Writer's Relief we recommend that a writer query at least 100 agents before going back to the drawing board.

Some editors and literary agents will recommend that a writer only query a handful of agencies. That's not necessarily bad advice—but what if it doesn't pan out? We cannot tell you the number of times we've seen a writer on the brink of giving up after making his or her 99th submission—only to have the 100th submission hit its target.

At Writer's Relief, we help our clients make approximately 100 submissions to literary agencies over a period of many months. Then, if nothing works, we schedule a meeting with our client to discuss the next step. Revision? A new project? Trying to get excerpts published? Self-publishing? There are many options.

Network Up: How And Where To Meet Literary Agents In Person (Or "Virtually" In Person)

In the old days, the publishing industry tended to be much more closed off to creative writers. These days, it is relatively easy to meet literary agents by attending writing conferences in your area. Often, writing groups will pay literary agents to attend their conferences, to give lectures, and schedule "speed dating" sessions with individual writers.

At a writing conference you can sign up for a 10-minute session with a literary agent to make your pitch in person. Often, these personal interactions can lead literary agents to take a submission more seriously, because now he or she has a face to put with the name on the manuscript.

However, there is a new way to meet literary agents that does not involve leaving your house. The Internet—and social networking—has changed everything. Literary agents and editors can be found on the Web, and they're interested in connecting with you.

Where To Find Literary Agents:

1. Twitter. Lots of agents are tweeting. They tweet about industry news and work they have represented or are proud of. Twitter allows a writer to follow a potential agent without necessarily having to deal with the privacy controls of other social networks. So go ahead and follow your favorite agent—and if he or she posts about a new book deal, why not tweet a note of congratulations?

2. Blogs. A number of literary agents have blogs (you can find them by Googling "literary agent blog"). By commenting regularly, intelligently, and politely, you may catch a literary agent's eye. Establish yourself as someone worthy of attention, and you may find your submission floats to the top of the pile.

3. Online writing classes. Sometimes, literary agents and editors will teach online classes for various writing groups. Often, these classes aren't accredited and anyone can join. Not only will you meet literary agents and editors, you'll also learn a thing or two!

4. Facebook. Few literary agents will accept your friend request for access to a personal profile on Facebook. At Writer's Relief we have a thriving Facebook community of writers. But if you're hoping to network with literary agents, Facebook might not be the best place to start unless the agent in question has a public Facebook page that you can Like.

Tips For Successful Online Networking:

1. Keep any emails brief, friendly, and grammatically correct.

2. Don't stalk. Obviously. That's just scary.

3. Be positive. No tweeting about bellyaches and bad days at the office.

4. Keep it light.

5. Don't ask for favors. Really. Don't. Networking has to be about developing relationships first and foremost. Then, if it feels natural, go ahead and gently ask.

6. Don't demand people read too much of your creative writing. Posting too much of your writing online can say to an agent or editor, "This person can't get anyone else to publish his/her work."

7. Have an author website that people can visit to learn more about you and your current projects.

8. Be helpful.

9. Follow through with any promises you make.

10. Have fun! (If you're not having fun, people will know it. And nobody wants a spoilsport at the party.)

How To Interpret Submission Guidelines

Every literary agent posts his or her preferred submission guidelines. But there is some common, industry-specific lingo you'll need to know.

NOTE: Some of these terms refer to publishing short stories, poems, and personal essays in literary journals. But we are including the terms here because it will help to be familiar with them as you build individual publication credits before searching for a literary agent for your book.

Definitions And Explanations Of Words You'll Find On Submission Guidelines Pages

Multiple submissions: If you send multiple submissions, you're sending more than one submission to one single editor or literary agent (sending two books to one agent, for example, is a multiple submission). Literary agents rarely accept multiple submissions.

No attachments: Most literary agents want to receive their queries without attachments because of the risk of viruses.

Reading period: The time frame during which a literary magazine is open to reading submissions. Literary agents tend not to have reading periods because many of them read all year long. Some writers mistakenly believe that literary agents stop reading during the summer months—but this is not true. Summer can be a great time to find a literary agent for your book.

Response time: The time it will take for you to hear back about your submission. The response time varies from one market to the next, and from agent to agent. Some literary agents only respond if interested.

Simultaneous submissions: Submitting a given work or group of works (such as a novel or a short story) to many editors or agents at the same time.

Word count or page count: Most literary agents ask that novel or memoir be at least 50,000 words. Use the word count feature in your word processing program to find an estimate of your word count, and include the estimate on the first page of your manuscript. Some literary agents will ask that you send "no more than the first ten pages of your manuscript," in which case the word count is a bit flexible. That said, be sure you submit according to industry-standard format guidelines: 12-point, simple font (like Times New Roman), one-inch margins, double-spaced—you know, no funny stuff.

What Do These Phrases Mean?

"We do not accept genre fiction." If a literary journal or literary agency says it does not accept genre fiction, this means they do not accept work that could be classified among the commercial genres.

"Query only." If a literary agency requests "queries only," the agents will not look at manuscript pages of a book. Send only a one-page query letter.

"Requires exclusivity, the exclusive right to consider the manuscript, or the right of first refusal." If a literary agent wants an exclusive, it means he or she wants to be the only person considering your manuscript. We'll cover more on this later.

Red Flags: 6 Shortcuts Agents Will Use To Reject Your Book

Everybody knows the best way to get an agent request is to write well and target submissions well. But did you ever stop to wonder what red flags professional readers look for when they're slogging through piles and piles of manuscripts?

Think of it this way: When you're deciding whether or not you want to eat at a particular restaurant, you're going to glance at the menu quickly before you decide to read further and check out the individual appetizers, entrees, and desserts.

If you're a hardcore carnivore, you're probably going to see the words to-fu, tempeh, and seitan as red flags. No need to spend any more time looking at this menu! Let's go to a steak house!

People who are reading submissions (reading them until their eyes blur) also have shortcuts. They look for red flags. They (consciously or not) use them as signposts that mean "this might end up being a rejection."

Here at Writer's Relief, we are unable to accept every writer who wants to work with us. We typically turn away about 80% of the writers who apply to join our client list. That means we read a lot of submissions. While we read absolutely every single submission that is sent to us— often with multiple readers—we (like literary agencies) *do* notice signs that suggest a writer may not be a good fit.

Here are the MOST COMMON red flags we see in the submissions that our Review Board (usually but not necessarily always) ends up rejecting.

1. Did not follow submission guidelines. When a writer's submission is way outside of our submission guidelines, he or she may be (inadvertently) proclaiming:

- I don't feel like following guidelines.
- I am not taking this seriously.
- I am not able to follow the directions (this could be for any number of reasons, some of which are legitimate).

Some red flags are like the little ones that children wave at parades. But blatantly ignoring submission guidelines is a big red flag the size of a parachute. HINT: If you are going to break the rules when making a submission, it may help to explain why you're doing it. Readers are forgiving when they know what to forgive!

2. Formatting. Submit in a simple, common font with your name and page numbers on each page. The writing should stand out; the formatting should not.

3. Typos. Time and time again, we find typos in the first line of submissions. Even if it's just an out-of-place comma, those little faux pas are annoying to a reader who still has 90 more submissions to get through. Sure, we'll forgive a stray typo here and there. Nobody's prefect (get it?)! But a reader can only see so many misuses of the word "there" before starting to feel discouraged.

4. The word count isn't suitable for submission. We've seen "novels" that are too short (30,000 words), "novels" that are too long (285,000 words), and "short stories" that are too long as well (10,000 words). Inappropriate word counts are easy-to-spot red flags.

5. Lack of supplemental materials. At Writer's Relief, we like to get a sense of a writer's personality because we need to work closely with our clients. We like to cultivate good energy here in our office, and we prefer to work with writers who are as enthusiastic about what they do as we are about helping them do it!

BUT some writers will fail to include a bio. Or they'll write "I'm a writer" and leave it at that. Imagine if you were excited to learn about a writer's goals, interests, and history—but all he or she told you was "I like to write." Already the reader feels deflated even before he or she gets to the actual writing.

6. Writers who send us long, bitter diatribes. We see a number of writers who complain about how literary agents won't take them seriously, poetry editors hate rhyming poems, nobody understands, somebody who helped them self-publish a project gave them the run-around and now are entirely to blame for the failure of said project (never mind the writer's allergy to doing research *before* signing a contract).

Such writers wonder why they're getting rejected at every turn. It breaks our hearts. Seriously. We get it; it's a tough business. ALL writers have it tough at some point. But it's the writers who don't consider themselves victims and persevere who succeed.

The Green Light For Red Flags

Sometimes we come across a truly great writer who means well but just makes a few errors when submitting. Or we find a submission that is so compelling, the writer could have submitted in crayon and we wouldn't care. (NOTE: This is an imaginary scenario. We do not accept submissions in crayon—at least not from anyone over the age of three.)

The point is this: If you want to increase your chances of getting an agent request, consider how literary agents might use shortcuts to weed through submissions. Then, avoid hoisting your own red flags.

The 10 Most Common Ways Writers Botch Their Chances Of Getting A Great Literary Agent

1. Beginning your novel with long descriptions of the weather or the scenery. Avoid an "information dump" right off the bat, including drawn-out descriptions of the main character or backstory.

2. Beginning the story with a cliché. If it feels even mildly familiar, skip it.

3. Asking for a detailed critique of your submission. Literary agents can't do that.

4. Writing clueless query letters. Queries that brag, grovel, and show a lack of professional know-how are a no-go to literary agents.

5. Missing deadlines. Writers who promise a synopsis within a week should deliver.

6. Insisting on becoming "part of the process" in areas best left to other professionals. Writers should not push their cover art ideas on a literary agent or second-guess the agent's advice on legal contracts. There's a big difference between integrating yourself in the process in an intelligent, well-informed way—and being a royal pain.

7. Querying with inappropriate material. Agents who specifically represent one genre (Westerns) are annoyed by submissions of other genres (horror). Do your research or have Writer's Relief do it for you.

8. Being a prima donna. If you land a contract, this is not the time to become high maintenance.

9. Trying to get noticed with gimmicks. Agents aren't impressed by authors who write their queries with silver gel pens on black paper or who include a miniature doll to represent their main character.

10. Reacting immaturely to rejection. Blasting an agent for rejecting your novel by blogging about them will only tarnish your reputation as a serious and professional writer.

5 Submission Strategy Essentials For Landing Your Dream Agent

1. Get the look. If you want people to take you seriously, you've got to present yourself in a serious way. When making your submissions to agents and editors, skip the bright-colored paper, the "clever" query letter intros (editors get sick of them fast), the small photo of your face on the manuscript. Just be brief, straightforward, and businesslike. Also, follow industry-standard formatting and have your work proofread.

2. Write to the right people. A big mistake when making submissions is taking the "blanket" approach: wallpapering the whole country with your query letters. A few well-placed and specific queries truly mean much more than 50 that are almost well-placed. Queries that are almost well-targeted will almost get you published. Do the research (or hire someone who will) to make your submissions matter. (NOTE: We've found that writers who take this seriously tend to be more successful. Submitting selectively is a sign of a writer who knows what she or he is about. Selective writers put so much love into their manuscripts that they won't submit to just anyone. Selectiveness is a very good sign because it demonstrates the right attitude for success.)

3. Be the tortoise, not the hare. Make sending submissions part of your writing habit. Submitting your work in dribs and drabs is NOT a strategy; it's a crapshoot. Sustainable and steady wins the race. To a certain extent, submissions are a numbers game. Create a schedule to lock yourself into making submissions.

4. Organization is your friend. Some people are naturally well-organized but others are not. To truly make the most of your submissions, you need to keep track of who read what, who liked what (and why), who rejected what (and why), who wants to see more work from you, and who did or did not request an exclusive read of the whole manuscript. We won't sugarcoat this: It is a TON of work (that's why Writer's Relief takes on this burden for our clients). When the acceptance letters start coming in, you'll thank yourself for the extra effort.

5. Chin up! Last but not least, work to maintain a good attitude. Negative thinking, getting glum about rejections, and believing yourself less than worthy... It's easy to fall into those traps. Positive thinking takes real effort when you're getting bombarded by rejections (and you WILL get bombarded—it's part of the process). Start looking at your rejection letters as proof of your dedication, devotion, and all-around awesomeness. Attitude is often the only difference between a nobody and a rising star. Every rejection brings you closer to a success, so submit regularly and chip away at those numbers.

Part Four

After Submitting...
What Happens Next?

Solutions For Agent Requests, Rejections, And Uncertainties

Now That Your Submissions Are Being Considered...

Just because your submissions are out in the world does not mean that your work is done. In fact, many of the difficult decisions that you may encounter when you are trying to find a literary agent will happen *after* your submissions have already gone out.

Of course, the first thing you must do is prepare yourself to be patient. Some literary agents will reply to you immediately. Others will take months or more. Some will not reply at all.

Some will reply with questions for you or requests that could make you uncomfortable. It's important to be prepared. Fortunately, you have this book to help.

We will guide you through some of the sticky situations that can arise when you begin submitting your book to literary agents. But there's one thing to keep in mind about advice that you get from *anyone* regarding how to proceed with a literary agent: You must trust your instincts and make your own way.

Your situation is going to be unique, and while generalizations offering good advice can certainly be helpful when you're making a decision, ultimately you must make the decision that will be best for your particular situation. At Writer's Relief, we approach each client's problems, conundrums, and triumphs from a personal angle. You must do the same for yourself.

How To Follow Up With A Literary Agent

Being patient can be difficult when you haven't heard from a literary agent that you've queried. Let's tackle some of the common questions that arise when writers want to nudge a literary agent who has not responded to a query, proposal, or manuscript.

Is it okay to send a query or manuscript with a request for a signature upon delivery?

No. If you want Delivery Confirmation, don't make a literary agent (or anyone else in the agent's office) sign for your letter. Ask your local post office or other courier's office how you can get confirmation of delivery without a request for a signature.

Is it okay to ask a literary agent to confirm immediately that he or she received a query letter, proposal, or book manuscript?

Generally speaking, no—it's not okay to submit a query with a simultaneous request for confirmation of receipt. Of course, this poses problems for writers.

Some literary agents who accept email queries have adopted a policy of replying to queries only if they are interested in the project in question. That leaves the writer in a quandary: Wait and assume that no news is bad news? Or wait, and then follow up?

There's no right or wrong answer here. If you've waited a substantial period of time (at least three months), and you are really itching to write a follow-up, then at that point you may have nothing to lose. The literary agent will either confirm that you've been rejected or ask you to resend your query.

But we don't recommend immediately following up a query with a request for receipt confirmation. It's just bad form—and the literary agent will likely find it annoying.

Tip: Know what else will annoy literary agents? Asking them to go through some kind of anti-spam verification process in order to respond to your email. Not the best way to make friends.

What is the ideal amount of time to wait before following up with a literary agent?

While there is no rule about how long to wait before asking for an agent's opinion on your manuscript, the key is to consider how you would feel if you were a literary agent. If you're getting 500 query letters a month, impatient people annoy more than impress.

Some literary agents have guidelines on their websites that indicate how long to wait before making an inquiry. (For example: You may follow up on your submission after six weeks.) For those literary agencies that don't offer instructions, be as patient as possible. If you push an agent to read your query, he or she will read it all right—with the understanding that you are impatient and pushy.

Are there extenuating circumstances that make it okay to send a follow-up?

If you are in an unusual circumstance (especially a circumstance that pertains to having competition for your book), then a literary agent may be more open to a follow-up.

The best circumstance for following up with one literary agent is when another agent has requested your materials. It's more appropriate to say, "I'm following up with you because another agent has requested my complete manuscript, and I wanted to let you know" than it is to say, "I'm feeling anxious and want you to drop what you're doing and read my book."

How should you follow up with a literary agent?

More often than not, literary agents prefer to communicate via email, which allows them to read and reply at their own pace. It's rarely appropriate to call. And it's never appropriate to stop by in person—no matter how close you just happen to live to the literary agent in question.

When you do send a follow-up email, be polite and brief. Don't use a vague subject line like "My book." Instead, be specific:

SUBJECT: Joe Writer, follow-up, The Case of the Missing Facts

or better yet

SUBJECT: Joe Writer, follow-up, notice of manuscript request

The Hidden Language Of Literary Agent Rejection Letters

Rejection letters from literary agents can be discouraging—especially impersonal, one-line form letters. But rejection is an unavoidable part of the writing process. Creative writers should know how to interpret the information in rejection letters and then use this knowledge to improve their submissions.

First, let's look at the different types of rejection letters:

The Form Letter Rejection

A form letter rejection is easy to spot. This may be a short, generic note that reads something like, "Dear Writer—No thanks." Or "Dear Writer—Please try again."

There's not much to be learned from a blanket rejection letter. But some literary agencies do have "tiered" rejection letters: one form for writers they don't want to encourage; one for people who are good writers but who aren't a good fit; one for writers who are invited to submit again.

Some literary agents who do not use a form will simply send the work in question back with a handwritten note or short email that says something like, "Not for us."

Standard Phrases Used In Rejection Letters From Literary Agents:

- Cannot use it/accept it at this time
- Didn't pique my interest
- Didn't strike a chord
- Doesn't meet our needs
- Doesn't fit our plans
- Have to pass on this
- Isn't resonating with me/us
- Isn't something we'd like to pursue
- No room for more clients (unless truly compelling)
- Not a right fit
- Not exactly what we're looking for
- Not for us
- Not suitable for us
- Not quite right for my list

- We are not enthusiastic enough about this work
- We are not certain we could be effective in placing your work
- We are not right for your work
- We do not have a place/room for this

...and the list goes on!

If you receive a rejection letter with phrases like those above, be careful not to misinterpret it. A form letter doesn't mean you targeted your writing to the wrong agent. It doesn't mean you've made a mistake by sending your submission. A form letter, no matter what the exact phrasing, is a nice, generic way of saying no thanks.

The Personal Rejection Letter

When a literary agent has taken the time to include a comment about your submission, then you know it's a personalized rejection.

Even if the comment is a critique of your work, we recommend you consider resubmitting to any literary agent who cared enough about your work to offer a personal comment.

Send the agent a thank-you note, and if/when you resubmit, reference the comments from the original rejection.

An Invitation To Resubmit

Some literary agents always invite writers to submit again—it's part of their form rejection. But others make such an offer more cautiously.

- We invite you to submit more in the future.
- Do you have anything else we can consider? Please send.

Why, you may wonder, are you being rejected if the writing is so great?

A book may be rejected simply because the timing is off. Or your project was too similar to something else already in the works. Or the agent might believe you have talent and he or she is looking forward to seeing you develop it.

Either way, send a thank-you note and a new submission (when possible); and again, reference the agent's original comments in your query letter.

Close, But Not Quite

Often, writers get discouraged when they get too many "near misses." But there's a valuable lesson to be learned if you're receiving rejections that imply "close, but not quite."

Take the time to analyze any comments you've received. Is there a common thread (i.e., tired theme, flat characters, weak ending)?

However, when deciding to make revisions based on feedback, think carefully before you start taking every piece of advice thrown your way. Follow your heart and consider the comments thoughtfully—avoid knee-jerk reactions.

For example: If one agent writes, "You should have written this in first person," you may want to wait to hear if any other agents have the same comment before making such a drastic revision. It's important to trust your instincts.

Keep in mind that what one agent dislikes, another agent might enjoy! But if you receive multiple comments that critique the same elements, it may be time to revise.

Finally, if you're getting many nice rejections, reevaluate your submission strategy. Are you sending your query letters to the literary agencies who are truly best suited for your particular book? Even the "right" book will not find a home at the "wrong" literary agency.

Why do literary agents use form letters?

The fact is, agents receive too many submissions to provide a personal comment on each piece. Hence, form letters.

How should writers deal with rejection letters?

Writing is a business, and writers must remember that agents have nothing against them personally.

Agents' jobs depend on the choices they make, and if they don't feel the work will sell—or they simply don't feel any enthusiasm or passion for the book—they don't have time to argue or explain exactly why.

Literary agents have different tastes and interests, which is why writers should learn what they can from rejection letters and then keep submitting to find the agent who will love their work.

If you're struggling with rejection, check out our book *The Happy Writer: Your Secret Weapon Against Rejection, Dejection, Writer's Block, And The Emotional Pitfalls Of The Writing Life.* Find out more on our website's store.

The Best Thing You Can Do When A Literary Agent Requests Your Book

If a literary agent asks to read your entire manuscript, pat yourself on the back! Something in your book or novel piqued the agent's interest—not an easy thing to do. The literary agent believes you may have something that he or she could sell to an editor.

BUT—before you send your manuscript off to the agent, there are a few things to consider. You'll want to get the most mileage out of the agent's interest in your book. A savvy and diplomatic writer may be able to use one agent's request to stir up interest from other agents (but only if said writer is truly interested in a partnership with those other agents—otherwise, it's a waste of everyone's time).

Tips To Help You Decide How To Handle An Agent's Request For A Complete Manuscript:

Of course, the easiest thing to do is to simply send the manuscript ASAP, as per the agent's request. No questions asked.

But sometimes, consider this:

You may want to alert some of the other literary agents who are currently looking at your query letter that your manuscript is under consideration. You don't need to drop the names of the people who are reading your book, but by informing the other agents you queried that your full manuscript is currently being read by another agent, you may just get bumped to the top of the slush pile. After all, no literary agent wants to get scooped by a competitor.

Tip: Don't call. Agents hate that. Email is fine. State simply that you want to let so-and-so know that another literary agency has requested your complete manuscript and that you want to extend the courtesy of informing him/her.

If your potential literary agent later requests an exclusive read, then you might have a little bit more difficulty fulfilling the agent's request to see your manuscript.

What To Do When A Literary Agent Requests An *Exclusive* Read Of Your Manuscript

Sometimes, when a writer sends a query off to a literary agency, the agent will request an "exclusive"—that is, the privilege of reading a manuscript before any other literary agent is allowed to see it. An exclusive is a kind of "right of first refusal" for agents.

The word "exclusive" tends to make writers panic. *What if I grant an exclusive and another agent wants to read the book? What if I don't want to grant an exclusive because I'm holding out for some other agent? What if I've already given the manuscript to someone else before the request for an exclusive?*

In any of these situations, there's no reason to panic. In fact, you should be THRILLED to have such a great problem. If a reputable agent is intrigued enough to request an exclusive, you're in a good position. Congratulations!

Here are a few "problem" scenarios, and some steps you might take to resolve them. Keep in mind that every situation will be unique, so these recommendations cannot work as "one size fits all" solutions to your particular case. But they may help.

What if the first literary agent who wants to read my book asks for an exclusive?

If the first agent who requests your book wants a guarantee that you won't send it to anyone else until he or she is finished, there are a few things you should consider. First, evaluate your feelings about the agency. Is it your number one choice? If so, you may need to be flexible. While you do have the power to decline an agent's request for an exclusive, we recommend you consider granting an exclusive for two weeks only. Another option is to indicate to the agent that she or he is the first to request the complete manuscript, and while you cannot grant an exclusive read, you will keep the agent informed if any other literary agencies request the manuscript. This may be enough to put the agent at ease.

What if a literary agent asks for an exclusive, but there's already another agent reading the book?

If this happens, thank your lucky stars. It means there's a lot of interest in your book—and you can use that momentum to keep the enthusiasm going. Politely state that the response to the book has been very positive, and you're unable to grant an exclusive because another agency is already reading the book. Then be sure to (tactfully) go back and tell the first agent that another agent has put in a request.

How Do You Approach Big-Time Agents Who Have A Lot Of Rules And Demand Exclusives?

If you're querying a well-known, influential agent and he or she wants an exclusive, you may need to be prepared to agree or lose a potential deal. When you approach the bigger agencies (the ones that don't accept unsolicited queries, don't take unpublished writers, refuse simultaneous submissions, etc.), the rules of making submissions change.

In this particular scenario, you'll want to query just one agency at a time. If your top agent requests an exclusive, give it—and then stop sending out queries and be very patient. Why? Because if you continue to query agents after you've given your top agent an exclusive read, it's unprofessional to tell any others who request your book, "Can you wait until I hear back from someone I like better than you?" You'll ruin that deal faster than you can say *New York Times* best seller.

How To Send A Revised Book To An Agent Who Has Already Seen It

As writers, our work is never done. Some of us will spend years working on a book, and then, finally—once we think it's finished—we'll submit it to a literary agent. But just because you've sent out queries doesn't always mean the book stops evolving.

Often—once a project has been rejected—a writer will revise and revise until he or she thinks the book is a more attractive project. Then, it's time to resubmit. But what's the right way to go about resending your revised book?

As with so many things related to the publishing business—there are no "one size fits all" answers to difficult questions. Always do your research, follow guidelines, be courteous, and trust your professional intuition.

1. How To Resubmit To A Literary Agent

If you've written a novel, memoir, or proposal for a nonfiction book, and you've already sent your project to a literary agent for representation, it's not wrong to submit your project again; however, it's important to resubmit thoughtfully and with respect.

And that means learning to think like a literary agent.

When is it okay to resubmit a book project to a literary agent?

There are a number of good reasons you might consider resubmitting a query letter or manuscript:

- You have significantly revised.
- The market has become more favorable to your book genre.
- You have built up your professional writing bio since the last submission was made.
- Your project has been nominated for an award or received some other important accolade that indicates your project appeals to readers.
- You have reworked your query letter to be a more accurate representation of your work. NOTE: We are NOT suggesting that resubmitting a series of revised queries to find one that works is a good idea. However, if you felt your first attempt at a query

letter was perhaps a bit amateur, and you later revised the letter, then you may be in a good position to resubmit.

The bottom line: If there is a reason that your book is more attractive now than it was ten years ago (or even ten months ago), then it may be worthwhile to do a round of resubmissions.

2. How Long To Wait Before Resubmitting The Same Project To An Agent

The best way to handle this issue is a bit subjective. You'll need to trust your instincts. Obviously, it would not make sense to submit a project to a literary agent only a few weeks after that same project was rejected. A few months might be too short a time frame as well—but it depends on your particular circumstances and your correspondence with the agent in question.

But if a literary agent requested revisions in the rejection letter, then you probably should not wait overly long to resubmit. Once the revisions are done, resubmit the project to the agent who offered you the critique. Be sure to clearly mark the envelope or subject line with "requested material."

3. Whether Or Not To Mention In Your Query Letter That The Book Is Being Resubmitted

If you had a personal conversation (in print or on the phone) with an agent about your book, then you may want to point out that this is a revised resubmission.

Otherwise, we recommend starting your resubmissions as if you're presenting the book for the first time—a fresh, clean slate. We see no compelling reason a writer should indicate "this book has already been around the block and had no takers."

8 Questions To Ask If An Agent Offers You Representation

Has a literary agent offered to represent you and your book? Congratulations! The following is a list of questions to ask a literary agent while you're in the "getting to know you" stage.

Please note: Some of these questions may be answered on the agent's website or in other supporting materials. Don't ask questions that don't need to be asked if the information is already available to you!

1. How long have you been in business as a literary agent?

No one goes to school to learn how to be a literary agent, but experience within the publishing industry can give an agent the edge when it comes to selling your book. Agents profit from their intimate understanding of editors' reading preferences, so you'll want someone who has strong connections. That said, don't write off new agents. New agents are always hungry for manuscripts, so if you connect with a new agent at an established literary agency, you both may benefit from the partnership. Just be sure to do your homework and ask the right questions!

2. What is your experience with this particular book genre?

An agent who only handles romance novels might not have the right contacts to shop a thriller around. While the agent might be trying to broaden his or her genre horizons, you have to ask yourself if you want your book to be the guinea pig. If the agent's enthusiasm is strong, it might be to your benefit to work with the agent in a genre that he or she doesn't historically represent. Again, weigh the pros and cons by getting all the necessary information before you make a decision.

3. Who will be handling my work within the agency?

Make sure you know who will be familiar with your book and to whom you can go if you have any questions down the road. Some agents at bigger companies will assign you to an assistant or a junior agent rather than represent your book personally. However, if you're working with a boutique agency, you'll probably be working with the agent you queried. Just be sure you know!

4. What is your plan for my book?

You should always know what an agent has in mind for your book, including how the book will be positioned within the larger market and if there is a possibility of selling secondary rights (film, audio, electronic, etc.).

5. How often will I be updated on what you're doing on my behalf?

No one should do anything with your book that you are not aware of. Writers put a lot of trust in their agents, but what's at stake is your career. Communication is crucial. Does your prospective agent prefer email correspondence or a phone call for a quick chat every once in a while? Find out ahead of time.

6. Are you a member of the Association of Authors' Representation (AAR)?

You may take heart in knowing that your agent is part of the AAR; however, if an agent is NOT an AAR member, you probably shouldn't consider it a deal breaker. The important thing is that the agent is in line with the AAR's requirements for ethics and handling clients' funds.

7. What are your commission rates?

We have already reviewed standard commissions for literary agents. Be sure you ask, just in case.

8. How will you be involved in my ongoing career?

Every agent has a different approach to building an author's career: Some are collaborators (working with authors on their projects in a very hands-on way by offering critique), while others are more aggressively involved in the negotiation process. Ask your potential agent how he or she likes to work with clients.

5 Tips To Get The Inside Scoop On A Literary Agent

When researching literary agencies, most writers decide to query a literary agent based on the information in a book of market listings (a compilation in which agents will briefly describe their experience and their literary wish lists).

But if a literary agent that you queried has reached out to you—either to request your complete manuscript or to make you an offer of representation—then it's time for a deeper investigation into your potential partner.

The obvious first step to take if you want to learn more about a particular literary agency is to visit that agent's website and ask the questions we have suggested.

But if you want to know about a literary agent's reputation within the larger publishing community, it's up to you to uncover the behind-the-scenes scoop. Put on your amateur sleuth hat, and let's start digging up clues!

Sign up for Publisher's Marketplace. Publisher's Marketplace is a website where literary agents, writers, and editors post information about book deals that have been successfully negotiated. This part of the website is not free, but anyone can join. (publishersmarketplace.com)

While not every single literary agent will post a book deal on Publisher's Marketplace, many literary agents and editors do check in regularly. You can do the same: Log in and do a search on your potential literary agent. Has the agent been active? For how long? And how recently? How many book deals has he or she done? Is he or she a new literary agent?

Dig deeper online. Many writers Google the name of their potential literary agent, skim the first page of results, and stop there. But you can often find more information about a literary agent when you dig deeper—into the second, third, and fourth pages of your search engine results.

You may find other writers talking about your potential agent in a forum or message board. You may discover blog interviews or commentaries. You could also discover interviews with writers who are represented by your potential literary agency. Every little bit of information helps when you are trying to decide whether or not a certain literary agent is right for you.

Visit Preditors And Editors. Preditors And Editors is a central hub where writers can share complaints or grievances about publishing industry professionals. Check to see if there are any complaints against your potential literary agent. (pred-ed.com)

Ask around. If you are involved in a writing group or association, ask other members what they know about the literary agent you are considering. But remember: If the writer you are talking to does not have direct experience with the literary agent in question and is simply repeating what he or she has heard, take the information with a grain of salt.

In a best-case scenario, you will be able to connect with another writer who has worked directly with the literary agent in question. But if you're hearing whispers from *many* different writers that your potential agent is not aboveboard, you might want to heed the warnings.

Go to a writing conference. Many literary agents make appearances at writing conferences. If possible, find out where your potential literary agent will be speaking or appearing, and then make plans to attend. If your potential literary agent is speaking at a well-known and reputable writing conference, the odds are good that the agent is well-known and reputable. Visit our website for a great list of writing conferences.

Remember To Look At The Big Picture

Talking to one writer or visiting one website will not give you a complete perspective of your future literary agent. You could meet one writer who has had a fabulous experience with your agent, and another who describes the partnership as "so-so." Instead, take a multipronged approach: Gather as much information as you can from multiple sources. Only then will you be ready to make one of the most important decisions of your life!

Is It Okay To Settle For An Agent Who Is Not Your Top Choice?

At Writer's Relief, we meet many writers who have dreams of landing a pie-in-the-sky literary agent for their book or novel. But let's face it—that doesn't always happen. Sometimes, a writer is offered representation from a literary agency that isn't in their top tier. Other times, a writer will receive an offer from a literary agent who is just starting out or who has a solid but not spectacular reputation. The question is always the same: Is a good literary agent—or an okay agent—good enough?

Each situation is different. Many variables play into a writer's ability to get the agent of his or her dreams—including the quality of the writing, demand for the type of work in question, and the writer's personality. But we hope our suggestions will help you make a good decision about your specific situation.

Before You Start Querying Literary Agents

If you've done your homework and you know that there are a handful of literary agencies who would be perfect for your book, then we recommend you query those few agents before you begin querying your B-list agents. After you've queried your favorites and waited an appropriate amount of time, you can move on to querying others. This will save you from having the potential problem—later on—of receiving an offer from your B list when you're still waiting for a response from your favorite agent.

Getting Real About Good Literary Agents

If your top first-choice agents show no interest in your work, don't lose faith. Keep in mind that a B-list agent might actually be a great literary agent who has the workhorse reputation and ethic that it takes to get the job done for you. Literary agents who are striving to build great reputations on the foundation of good reputations will often be passionate advocates for your writing—perhaps more passionate than if you were to be represented by an agent who has a "been there, done that" attitude.

How To Respond To A Not-So-Great Agency

If you've received an offer from a literary agent that you suspect does not have a sound reputation and ethic, we recommend that you steer clear.

But keep in mind that there are literary agents who might be set up legitimately and ethically, but who don't yet have the connections, talent, reputation, and track record that it can take to negotiate good contracts with reputable publishing houses. You may want to proceed, but do so cautiously.

Remember: If a literary agent makes an offer to you, YOU are the one with the goods (the manuscript), and you don't have to agree to anything you don't want to agree to.

Take your time, ask questions, and let the other literary agents (those you prefer) know that you've had an offer of representation and that you would like a response regarding your manuscript within the next week. If you don't get any bites, you might consider going with the literary agent who made the offer. Just be sure everything's legit and in your best interest.

How To Put A Literary Agent On Hold

Some writers want to tell a literary agent, "Can you hold that thought while I wait to hear back from my first-choice agent?" It's risky to do this, but not necessarily unwise, depending on the situation.

After speaking with the literary agent about his or her offer and seriously considering the situation, you can politely tell the agent you need some time to think about it (you might not want to mention that you are following up with other agents—but it's up to you). A good agent will probably put some pressure on you to decide—agents are salespeople to an extent—but will hopefully also respect your wishes.

And if the agent in question is insulted and reacts with an "it's now or never" ultimatum, then it's up to you to decide how important chemistry is in your relationship. True, the literary agent might rescind his or her offer if you ask for more time—but we wonder: Would you want to work with an agent who puts so much pressure on his or her clients?

Finally, remember that some literary agents are busy enough without adding you to their client list. They assume (rightly, we hope) that you've done your homework before querying and you feel they could be a good fit for your work. Because of this, some agents will expect an immediate yes or no answer: They may not be inclined to take on an author who seems like he or she is on the fence.

There Are No Easy Answers

Because each writer is different and each writer has his or her own goals, we can't give you a "one size fits all" answer to the question of "should you settle when it comes to signing with a literary agent?" However, we can pose some questions that may help you to make an informed choice. By considering your answers to these questions, you might be able to determine how you really feel about your second-choice literary agent:

1. Have you truly queried a good number of the appropriate and reputable agents for your particular book genre? If not, are you sure you're ready to settle?

2. On a scale of one to ten (ten being most important), how important is mutual respect and trust in a writer-agent relationship? How does that apply to your situation with your potential agent? Do the scales tip slightly one way or the other? Now—what number would you assign for how much you trust the agent in question? Is there a big disparity between how much you want to trust and how much you actually do?

3. Would you prefer to have an agent try to sell your book, and then, if it doesn't work, you'll self-publish? Or would you rather just self-publish now because you're eager to see the work in print?

4. Is it very important to you to have a book that does well with national audiences? If so, would you consider revising and querying literary agents again—especially if you had any "close call" manuscript requests with literary agents you really loved?

Signing The Dotted Line: What You Must Know Before You Agree

A literary agent will negotiate contracts for you with publishers. But who is going to negotiate a contract with a literary agency for you? Many writers know what to do when a literary agent requests a manuscript. But few have taken the proactive step of understanding literary agent contracts before a contract is offered.

As for writers who *do* know their stuff even before they're offered a contract…well, we think that's a pretty good indicator of future success. So use this book to learn what you're getting into before you get yourself into it.

If a literary agent offers you a contract, which legal terms and phrases should you look out for? Which terms are negotiable, and which ones aren't? If the agent does not sell your book, how does the law say that you should part ways?

If you don't understand a contract's terms, don't sign it until you do. Never hesitate to show the contract to an attorney. We reiterate: Contracts typically favor the person who drafted them.

There are many issues and contract terms we could discuss, but these key provisions and the essential vocabulary should get you started. While we can't (and don't) offer legal advice, Writer's Relief submission strategists provide our clients with much-needed information about reputable agents.

The Anatomy Of A Literary Agency Contract

When you sign with a literary agency, consider the contract (or agreement) that bears your signature to be the owner's manual for your relationship with the agent. The terms under which the literary agency operates—everything from how and when you are paid to how and when you can sever your agreement—are governed by your literary agency contract.

We could spend a lot of time talking about the infinite details of a literary agency contract. There are many books available to writers about intellectual property law and publishing industry agreements.

In order to get you started, we are simply going to touch on the main parts of a literary agency contract. This will help explain what you can expect from your future partnership.

Keep in mind that all literary agencies are different and may have different contracts. A few literary agents may not use a written contract at all (but we recommend that you consider these agencies with caution).

The Parts Of The Literary Agency Contract

1. The parties involved. The first clause of your literary agent contract simply states that you and your literary agent(s) are drawing up the agreement.

2. Representation. The next clause often sets out the terms of representation—that your literary agent has the exclusive right to represent your interests to publishing houses and other companies and to negotiate on your behalf.

3. Term of contract. Most literary agent contracts are in full effect for 12 months. Does that mean your agent will ditch you in a year? Not necessarily. This can seem a little confusing at first, but bear with us as we explain further.

4. Commission. As stated previously, the standard commission for a first rights sale is 15%, and foreign rights are usually 20%.

5. Renewal. Most literary agency contracts stipulate that the terms of the contract are automatically renewed once every 12 months unless they are terminated. In other words, even though your contract is technically only for 12 months, the terms of your contract will automatically renew unless you put a stop to it by terminating the agreement.

6. Termination. Most literary agency contracts request 60 days' written notice prior to termination. Also, many literary agents will retain the right to commissions earned based on any work they did on your behalf.

Your literary agent has a "standard" contract. But if you feel uncomfortable with any concept or terminology, feel free to ask for changes. Most literary agents expect that you might ask for a change or two.

If you're not sure what something means, trust your instincts and go searching for more details. If your future agent gives you a very clear explanation of what a given phrase will mean to your career, then you may feel comfortable moving on. However, you may want to ask a literary attorney to review your literary agency contract in order to make sure that you are protected.

Ideally, your literary agent is on your team and will look out for your best interests. But it's always good to get a professional opinion when you have so much at stake.

7 Dangers To Avoid In A Literary Agency Contract

Some writers are offered an agreement from a literary agency and decide to simply "sign on the dotted line" without fully understanding what's at stake. They might take this approach because they have an implicit trust in their future literary agent. Others are overcome by emotion and are not thinking clearly.

Before you sign a contract with a literary agent, here are seven things to watch out for:

1. What exactly will your literary agent represent? Some literary agents will demand the right to represent absolutely everything that you write, from shopping lists to epic novels. Other literary agents will ask to represent one particular genre of book (such as "full-length science-fiction novels"). Whatever the case, make sure you understand exactly what your agent is asking to represent.

2. Is the termination clause clear and pro-writer? The termination clause should protect *you*: You should not have to "show cause" if you want to sever your relationship with your agent. Be certain that you understand the process for terminating your agreement before you sign.

3. What exactly will you be asked to pay for? If your literary agent charges you a "signing fee" or if he or she asks you for a sum of money up front to cover the cost of postage and phone calls, that's your cue to start doing a lot more research about the agent in question.

4. Are the commission rates crystal clear? Do you understand what percentage of sales your agent will claim as commission? Keep in mind that if you do sell your book, you might also sell subsidiary rights (like the right to adapt your book into a movie). Be sure that you understand what kind of commission your literary agent will take and what kind of commission any partner agencies may claim.

5. How soon will you receive your money? Most literary agencies act as trustees for their clients. Instead of paying you directly, a publisher will pay your literary agent—who will then cut you a check (minus commission). Your literary agent contract should state how quickly you can expect your money after your literary agency has received it.

6. Will you be able to see a clear accounting? Your literary agent should send you the proper tax forms every year and should also, upon request, furnish you with a list of expenses incurred on your behalf (especially if they are charging you for things like postage and phone calls).

7. Is the agent asking for perpetual representation? Some literary agents will ask for the right to permanently represent a book that they worked on for you—as opposed to asking for the right to represent it *only* for the duration of your publishing contract or your partnership with the agency. Do not grant a right of perpetual representation.

Do You Trust Your Literary Agent?

Your literary agent is going to be your advocate. If negotiating a contract with your literary agent feels uncomfortable, or if you get the sense that your agent is not communicating with you accurately and fairly, you might want to take that as a warning sign. It may be time to head in a different direction.

And remember: Don't be afraid of negotiating or asking questions about your literary agency contract. You might thank yourself later down the line!

The Top 5 Tips For Negotiating Your Literary Agency Contract

5. Don't assume you know everything or that the contract writer knows best. Some writers assume that the lawyer who wrote the contract they're about to sign obviously knows best about the situation. But as a writer, you must be your own advocate.

Remember: Don't let an *If it were important, I would already know it* attitude cloud your judgment. And don't assume the contract writer is looking out for your concerns. When in doubt, hire a literary lawyer who is an expert and who will specifically look out for your best interests.

4. Don't be overly trusting. It's only natural that a writer who is flattered by being offered a contract of any sort might be inclined to trust the person offering the contract. After all, if an agency is smart enough to see that your writing is worth a contract, doesn't that make them implicitly better and more trustworthy than the agencies that didn't offer a contract?

Remember: It's easy to say "I wouldn't think that" when you aren't in that situation. Just be aware that many writers make the mistake of being too trustworthy when entering into an agreement. A healthy amount of caution, even skepticism, is important to your writing career.

If you weren't offered a written contract and were instead offered a handshake deal, remember that it's okay to ask for something in writing.

3. Don't rush and don't allow yourself to be rushed. When you're offered a contract, it's tempting to fall in line quickly, agree to everything, and give in to the urge to hurry the process along. Add that to the pressure from an agent to sign the contract now, now, now, and you've got a recipe for disaster.

Remember: You can take your time. Did it take years to write your book? If so, what's a few days more? Patience in all things related to writing helps.

2. Don't let gratitude turn you into a doormat. Some authors are ignored for years. So when they finally are offered a crumb of attention from an agent, it can be easy to become overly agreeable. This can lead a writer to agree to terms that aren't necessarily in his or her favor.

Remember: You can be grateful and glad without agreeing to everything. If you feel uncomfortable about an element of your contract, discuss it. You and your literary agent want the same thing: to come to an agreement that you BOTH can feel comfortable about for a long time. Give your agent the benefit of the doubt, and don't be embarrassed to bring up any terms that make you feel uncomfortable. If you receive an unprofessional or insensitive response, then you'll know it's time to head in a different direction.

1. You have the power in a negotiation. If you've been offered a contract, it's because you hold the rights to a commodity that's desirable. That means the ball's in your court—to an extent.

Agents and publishing professionals who have been in the business for years can be intimidating to a new writer. And intimidation, coupled with intense emotions, can lead a writer down a slippery path.

So take your time, step back, and remember: Nobody but you owns your writing. And nobody can replace you. You are in a unique position, and you deserve to negotiate a contract that works in your favor.

Then, when everything's done, congratulate yourself on getting a literary agent!

Part Five

Trouble In Paradise

How To Keep, Nudge, Encourage,
Or (Yikes!) Fire Your Literary Agent

When The Bloom Is Off The Rose...

A relationship with a literary agent is like any relationship: Some partnerships are successful; some leave both parties miserable. Some relationships can be saved; some have to be respectfully dissolved.

As a writer, you are in charge of your own future. So you'll need to know when you should try to salvage a broken relationship or when you should simply move on.

Not Getting Enough Attention From Your Literary Agent?

Do you feel like you're being ignored by your literary agent? Wondering if your manuscript is at the bottom of your literary agent's priority list? Is your agent ignoring your emails and phone calls? Or do you simply feel that your agent is not giving enough attention to your writing career?

Why Literary Agents Ignore Their Clients

Before you decide that your literary agent is ignoring you, be sure that you are accurate in your perception. Remember: While writing certainly can be a business, it's also extremely personal. And that can lead writers to misinterpret innocent behaviors as insults and slights against them.

That said, sometimes literary agents do fail their clients. Some agents agree to represent more clients than they can handle and provide only a minimum amount of support, casting a wide net in hopes that one of their clients will turn out to be a best seller.

Other literary agents take on fewer writers and spend a lot more time developing their clients' careers—but these agents also might be the first to drop a writer who isn't making money, since the agency is assuming a risk by their time investment.

Signs That Your Literary Agent May Be Ignoring You

- The agent does not return your phone calls.
- The agent takes a long time to return your emails.
- When the agent does return your email or phone call, he or she often seems rushed, distracted, and disinterested.
- The agent does not answer your questions thoroughly.
- The literary agent does not seem excited about you or enthusiastic about your work.
- The literary agent has promised to send out your manuscript or to return a critique to you but has failed to do so in a timely fashion.
- The literary agent has neglected to follow up with publishers and editors about your book.

What To Do If You Want More Attention From Your Literary Agent

If your literary agent really is too busy for you, there might not be a lot you can do to change the situation. But there are some things to try.

Get more flies with honey. By being a good client, you'll be more likely to find yourself prioritized. So what does it mean to be a good client? First, you must have a really fabulous book that is the complete package.

Second, you should be patient, polite, and genuinely caring. Make the effort to show who you are on a personal level: Send over a meaningful gift during the holidays or send a note expressing how excited and grateful you are that your agent takes such good care of you.

Try to demonstrate that you are accommodating your agent's tardiness. In your emails and correspondence, be kind and polite, noting that you understand that your agent is busy, that there's a lot going on, but that you would truly appreciate a response as soon as possible. By acknowledging that the agent is busy, you show that you respect and appreciate the work he or she is doing on your behalf.

Ask for a deadline. If your agent promises to read your manuscript and give you feedback, ask for a deadline on the grounds that you will need to shuffle your work schedule in order to dedicate your time to forthcoming revisions.

Plus, keep in mind that if you are going to ask your agent to meet a deadline, you must also be prepared to do the same thing. Don't blow your deadlines.

It's not you, it's me. If you are a good client and are doing everything you can do to help your career take off, then it may be time to tackle the situation head-on. Ask your agent for a phone call, and be sure to keep the tone friendly and upbeat: *I know you're a really fantastic agent. I'm so lucky to be working with you. I'm wondering if there's anything that I can do to make it easier for you to reply to me more quickly. How do you prefer to be contacted? Is there anything that I can do to help make this process easier for both of us?*

When you're really fed up... If you've tried being nice and it's gotten you nowhere, it may be time to get tough. You absolutely should be the first advocate for your own writing: If your agent is not getting the job done, then you need to find one who will. Express your concerns and disappointment in moderate and professional terms. And then, if you need to, be prepared to walk away.

The 6 Worst Things To Say To Your Literary Agent

When you're at a writing conference or chatting on the phone, it can be easy to fall into a sense of camaraderie with others—especially your literary agent. Many authors have the opportunity to meet their literary advocates only once or twice a year at a conference, so it's important to make the most of that time.

With any luck, you'll find that you have a lot of immediate chemistry with your agent, even if you've never met before. After all, you became connected because you both love a certain kind of book. You already have a lot in common.

That said, take precautions to remember that your agent is a professional acquaintance, not a close friend!

6 Things Never To Say To Your Literary Agent

1. "I think I had one too many to drinks!" (And yes, that typo is intentional.) Having one drink while you're at the bar chatting with your literary agent is not necessarily a bad idea. Having three drinks or more may cause a problem. At writing conferences, formalities tend to break down when the bar opens up. But even if other attendees are being liberal with their libations, it's best to take a measured approach. You don't want to appear unprofessional.

2. "Let me tell you what I heard about so-and-so." It's important never to take an opportunity with your agent to bad-mouth anyone else in the publishing industry. You should never spread gossip. Don't lie about your experiences with someone—keep in mind that it really is a small world.

3. "I'm not feeling very optimistic about all of this." If you are not excited about your prospects, your literary agent could begin to feel the same way. You are the person who is driving your career: Almost everything that happens ripples out from you. It's okay to express concern about very specific elements of your career; your agent is there to listen and help. But it's best to leave an agent with a sense of your positive energy about your writing—as opposed to your negative outlook and disappointment.

4. "Didn't I tell you that I already self-published a new book three months ago?" If you are planning on having anything to do with self-publishing—whether you are self-publishing a book that you one day hope will be picked up by a traditional publisher, or you are self-publishing a novella to go alongside another book—you should discuss it with your agent *before* you release the book. Your literary agent is your partner and will want to be kept apprised about *all* the elements of your writing career, from awards, to interviews, to new releases!

5. "I would work harder if I were making more money writing books." The last thing that your literary agent wants to hear is that you became a writer for the money. While the publishing industry does focus on profit, most people do not join the ranks of literary agents, editors, and writers because they are interested in making a fortune. They do it for love of the written word. And most of them want to know that your primary goal is to fulfill a passion, as opposed to make a buck.

6. "I'll do more (fill in blank here) once I can quit my day job." Most literary agents recognize phrases like this for what they are: not-so-subtle implications that the agent has failed to procure for his or her client the coveted lifestyle of a full-time writer. Your literary agent knows that you probably do want to quit your day job. There's no need to state the obvious.

Your Literary Agent Does Want To Be Your Friend And Confidant

It's important to have a good relationship with your literary agent. And we hope you will not feel self-conscious or limited in what you can discuss. Generally speaking, if you keep the conversation positive, you'll be fine!

The 10 Signs That It's Time To Say Good-Bye To Your Literary Agent

It's not easy to make the decision to leave your literary agency. No writer wants to fire a literary agent. Most of the time, literary agents and writers enter into their partnerships with lots of enthusiasm and optimism. Most writers would rather try to work out any problems with their current agent than start the entire process of finding literary agent representation all over again.

However, sometimes the signs point toward firing a literary agent.

10 Signs That It's Time To Fire Your Literary Agent

1. Your literary agent does not return your emails or phone calls in a timely manner and does not respond to your expressions of concern.

2. Your agent has not fulfilled his or her promises.

3. Your agent is taking a very long time to submit your manuscript to editors.

4. Your agent has submitted your manuscript to editors, but has not kept you up to date regarding responses.

5. Your agent seems to be hiding information from you or dodging questions.

6. Your agent is charging you a lot of money and you're not really sure why.

7. Your agent is "bundling" (sending your book manuscript out in a packet of many manuscripts to one single editor, instead of sending one book to one editor at a time).

8. Your agent is not offering you any form of proof that your manuscript has been sent out, such as faxed responses on letterhead or forwarded emails (sometimes with email address removed for the editor's privacy).

9. You have a bad feeling about your agent.

10. When you speak with other writers about their literary agents, you are increasingly worried that your literary agent does not measure up.

Cut Your Losses: What Do You Stand To Gain Or Lose If You Fire Your Agent?

If you fire a bad literary agent, there's always the chance that a better literary agent might be just around the corner. Just keep in mind that if you do terminate a relationship with an agent, you may need to explain the situation at some point.

It's like quitting a job. When you leave one position and interview for another, your potential employer will want to know why you left. Keep the conversation positive—say that you were eager to connect with a literary agent who had more time to dedicate to your book.

You will also need to make a decision about whether or not to mention your prior literary agency in your new query letters. Some writers prefer not to mention having fired their prior literary agent in their initial query letter, preferring instead to bring up that topic only after another literary agent has shown some initial interest in the manuscript. This way, the writer doesn't have to fumble through explaining what might be a very complex situation in just a few sentences in a query.

Just know that if you fire your literary agent, you may need to explain your choice when querying other agents.

Breaking Up Is Hard To Do

Some writers hesitate to fire a literary agent on the grounds that any agent is better than none. However, if a literary agent is not an enthusiastic advocate for your writing, then he or she may do more harm than good.

Once an editor has reviewed your manuscript, that editor will not want to see it again—even if your literary agency changes. If your "bad" literary agent has already sent your book to the eight to twelve editors most likely to acquire it, then your new literary agent may find his or her hands are tied.

As a writer, you must stand up for your own writing and not rely on anyone else to do it for you. If that means you need to fire a literary agent who is not treating your work with the respect it deserves, then don't feel bad about your decision to part ways.

How To Fire Your Literary Agent

If you do decide to fire your literary agent, there are a few things you need to be prepared for.

First things first: You will need to refer to your literary agent contract to understand the ramifications of your decision. Every literary agency is different.

If your literary agent has already sent your manuscript to editors, that literary agency may hold the rights to take a commission from any sale that results from the work that was already done on your behalf.

The new agent representing you *can* send the book to editors who haven't seen it yet provided you still hold the copyright. Your new agent will be able to take a commission on any sales produced by his or her efforts.

The rule of thumb is simple: The agent who did the work to make the original sale often gets the money (and, depending on the agency, handles all negotiations on your behalf). Hopefully your new literary agent will be able to smooth things over.

How To Fire Your Literary Agent

Check your contract. Your contract may stipulate the method of termination. Most literary agents require 60 days' written notice. Some will require a letter; for others, email is acceptable. Be sure that you follow the terms of your contract so there can be no question later on of the termination.

Send a letter. If you do not have a contract, send a tracked certified letter asking the agent to stop all work on your behalf. Say that you are terminating the partnership due to professional incompatibility.

Ask for a list. Request the names of specific editors who have considered or are still considering your manuscript. Some literary agents may be reluctant to give you this information because they are worried that you will directly contact the editor about the submission, which is not an industry-standard practice. But you are entitled to know what work has been done on your behalf. Also, if you plan to submit your book anywhere in the future, you will need to know where it has already been sent.

Consider making a phone call. Before sending your literary agent an email or certified letter, you may want to give the agent a call and let him or her know about your intentions. You do not need to go into the details of why you are severing the relationship. You can simply say, "I have decided to head in another direction. Thank you for everything that you've done."

If the agent demands to know more about why you are parting ways, be honest: Say that there has not been good communication or that you had different visions. No reason to get too specific—that's when feelings get hurt.

Be nice. Even if you despise your literary agent and feel resentful for a job badly done, be as kind and professional as possible. Remember: You may end up working with this literary agent again. Plus, when you do query new literary agents, there is always the possibility that your old agent and future agent may know each other and chat about you. So be sure that you never burn your bridges!

Don't Be Scared; Just Be Professional

It's never an easy decision to fire a literary agent. But if you have to do it, you'll sleep better knowing that you were courteous and respectful. We've said it before and we'll say it again: As a writer, you are your own best advocate. So don't be afraid to make the tough decisions.

Part Six

Special Considerations

New Paths To Traditional Publishing

New Ways Into Traditional Publishing

While most writers continue to use the time-honored route of having a literary agent help them publish a book, there are many new and alternate avenues to traditional publication.

In the next section, we're going to look at alternative paths to getting a literary agent and a book deal.

How Publishing An Excerpt Could Land You A Literary Agent

If you've written a book and are trying to have it published, consider this strategy to get literary agents and editors excited about your book:

Publish an excerpt.

That's right. Create a stand-alone short story or essay from your book.

Creating a short story or essay from your manuscript may seem time-consuming and counterproductive, but many writers have used this strategy with excellent results. Often, when you turn to the first pages of a book, you'll notice in the copyright section that the publisher wishes to acknowledge other small presses that previously printed selections from the book. Professional writers will frequently convert the first chapter of a book into a story or essay and then publish it in a literary magazine years before the book is even done.

But, you're thinking, *how can I turn part of my book into an excerpt?*

A short story or essay is easiest to place when it is shorter than 3,500 words. If you decide to create some stand-alone prose from within your book, keep in mind that you are allowed to revise your text. Your short story does not need to match word for word the portion of your book that it's based on. Feel free to play with your prose in order to give your excerpt the best shape for the medium. Also, if you'd like to write a story that is very loosely based on an event in your book—or maybe even a spin-off—that's fine too. The point is to be able to say in your query letter:

My story "Footsteps In The Hall," which is [based on/excerpted from] my book The Monster Keeper, *was published in* The Name-of-Magazine-Here Review.

There are a number of reasons excerpts can get you where you want to go.

Book excerpts generate enthusiasm. When a literary agent or editor sees that a portion of your book has been published in a reputable literary magazine, you could be bumped to the front of the line. Literary agents and editors like to see that you are actively publishing—and it's even better if what you're publishing is from the book that you're pitching.

Published excerpts indicate that there is a preexisting audience. When you publish an excerpt, you show that there is already interest out there for your writing. You indicate that the masses are ready and eager for a writer like you. And since the literary agent doesn't have to try to figure out how to position your book within the larger market, then you just might strike gold.

Excerpts build up your bio. We've already discussed how important it can be to build up your bio when you're approaching literary agents with a book project. Publishing an excerpt of your book demonstrates that you are a writer who is serious, professional, and capable.

Literary agents read magazines. Many of our clients have been approached by reputable literary agents who read something the client wrote in a magazine or literary journal. Literary agents often seek out new clients in their favorite publications.

Publishing Excerpts By Genre

If you are writing literary or mainstream fiction, or if you're writing essays as part of a memoir, there are countless literary journals and magazines available to you. For more information about where to find literary journals and how to submit to them, please visit our website.

If you are writing prescriptive nonfiction, you may want to target commercial magazines that speak directly to your audience. For example: If you're writing a nonfiction book about dieting, you may want to pitch a short article based on a topic in your book to a magazine about health.

Self-Publishing To Get A Traditional Publisher's Attention

Often, writers email us with variations on the same question: How can I get a literary agent for a self-published book? Their emails read something like this:

Dear Writer's Relief,

I self-published my book [enter number of months ago] and now I'm [A) not happy with my publishing company or distribution, B) disappointed because I'm not getting any sales of my self-published book, and/or C) thinking of expanding my already successful efforts by getting a literary agent and a traditional publisher for my self-published book]. Can you please tell me whether or not I can send my self-published book to literary agents?

Sincerely,

A Concerned Writer

While each author who has self-published is in a unique situation and there is no single answer for every writer, it is possible to submit your self-published book to literary agents.

If you do want to transition from self-publishing to traditional publishing, here are some tips for getting a literary agent:

1. Be as positive as you can be about your self-publishing experience. If you chose that route, be sure to demonstrate that your choice was deliberate, educated, and professional (hopefully it was!). You don't want to come off as the kind of person who doesn't look before she or he leaps.

2. Emphasize the success of your book by citing sales, quotes, and media coverage, if possible. Just be sure that any endorsements or quotes come from reputable, respected sources (not from random reviewers on book retailer websites or from your relatives).

3. Be sure you hold all rights to your book. You can't offer publishing rights if you don't own them.

4. Don't expect to use your own cover art, title, layout, etc. When you transition to a traditional publisher, you need to be prepared to give up much of your autonomy.

5. Be honest. If you find yourself in serious talks with an agent, don't hide your self-publishing history. Agents will look you up online.

6. Be prepared to remove your book from Amazon and other online retailers. If you sell your book to a traditional publisher, you don't want to undercut their sales. You'll need to think about whether or not you want to "freeze" your book sales before you attempt to get an agent or editor. A freeze will cut into your sales, but it may also demonstrate a firm commitment to traditional publishing. Weigh the pros and cons before making your decision.

7. Don't mess with the system. Some writers have asked us if it's possible to sell SOME rights to a publisher, but keep others for themselves. While a few writers have managed to pull this off, most self-published authors find themselves in an "all or nothing" situation. Publishers develop rigorous ideas about how they want to market, and for that reason they generally require control over nearly all rights. If you hold some rights and the publisher holds some rights, you will set yourself up as a competitor against your publisher.

8. Don't query with your bound, finished book. Query with plain old 8.5" x 11" formatted pages when necessary—as if the book had not been typeset and bound. Always follow agents' submission guidelines.

9. If you're querying literary agents for the first time with your book, it may be helpful to mention that. Some literary agents will suspect that self-published books are projects that failed to find homes at traditional publishing houses. If you've never queried before, your book may yet have a "freshness" factor worth mentioning.

Bonus Section

Build Your Author Platform

What's Your Big Picture?

Your Author Platform: Put Yourself In A Position To Shine

Literary agents and editors use the word *platform* within the publishing industry to talk about an author's relationship with his or her audience. Let's review the specifics of what a platform is, why literary agents and editors take them seriously, and whether or not you, as a writer, need one.

Author Platforms In Real Life

A platform involves many components: the author's expertise in the field that he or she is writing about; the author's preexisting popularity, notoriety, and status as a leader in his or her field; the author's personal, already established connection to the readership that will be interested in his or her book.

In short, a platform is the author's background within a given field that establishes him or her as the right person to publish (and sell) a book on the subject.

Most of the time, writers of self-help, how-to, or even biography proposals will need a strong platform. Literary agents do not place *quite* as intense an emphasis on platforms for novelists (and, sometimes, memoirists). However, the bigger your platform, the stronger your pitch.

What Is A Strong Platform? A Weak Platform?

Let's say you've written a nonfiction book proposal to publish a book about a brand-new diet: The Lima Bean Diet.

An Author Who Has A Strong Platform:

- Is a highly educated nutritionist with multiple degrees and special studies about lima beans
- Has written and published many peer-reviewed articles on lima beans in science journals
- Has written and published many popular weight-loss articles about lima beans in major commercial magazines
- Has a blog with a strong following of people who have had success with The Lima Bean Diet

- Has gained some preliminary media coverage (local TV spots, articles, interviews) that suggests The Lima Bean Diet is the next big thing
- Has led high-energy seminars all over the nation about The Lima Bean Diet and has a growing mailing list

An Author Who Has A Weak Platform:

- Has minimal or informal education in his or her field (relies on personal experience to prove The Lima Bean Diet works)
- Has published a few articles on The Lima Bean Diet with "underground" blogs, websites, and zines
- Has not published anything in commercial magazines or has published only in small-circulation periodicals
- Has a blog, but not many followers—and few followers are active
- Has a following of family and friends (with some friends of friends and some strangers)—but that's where it ends
- Has had little to no media coverage
- Has no reputation for being an expert, leads a couple of local seminars in libraries or health food stores

What Your Platform Means To A Literary Agent Or Editor

To make "big numbers" on a nonfiction book, a literary agent will look for an author who already has a built-in audience (an audience that depends on and trusts the author's expertise). Many writers believe that they "have a great idea for a book." And still more believe that their personal experiences alone make them an authority on their subject.

Nonfiction writing is especially competitive. If a literary agent "falls in love with" a project, he or she may be willing to work with an author to build up a platform (in order to impress an editor), but this happens very rarely. Instead, writers should build their own platform before querying an agent.

How To Build Up A Better Platform For Your Writing

1. Be (or become) an expert in your field.

2. Emphasize your experience or background if it pertains to your novel. For example, if you're a retired police officer and you've written a detective novel, it's definitely worth highlighting.

3. Establish a strong online presence via an author website, a blog, and social networking.

4. Submit short prose to literary journals and major commercial magazines to increase your publishing credits.

5. Offer to be an expert source for other people writing about your subject.

6. Present seminars and establish yourself as a speaker, if applicable.

7. Hire a publicist who can help with media exposure.

One last note: If you're writing a memoir, it helps to be high profile, but it's not necessary. Memoirs are not sold via proposal, and, therefore, their authors don't necessarily need a huge platform. For all intents and purposes, a memoir works like fiction: The book must be complete, not pitched via proposal.

Best-Case Scenario: The 5 Things Literary Agents Want To See In Your Author Platform

The most important element that will determine whether or not you will get a literary agent interested in your book is the strength of your story. But no manuscript is an island; there are many factors that inform a literary agent's decision about your submission. By building a strong author platform before you begin querying, you can make it easier for a literary agent to say *Yes!* to your book.

1. A professional author website. Your website is a central hub where agents, editors, and fans will go to learn more about you and your writing. In one form or another, all professional writers should have websites. By creating your author website even before your book is published, you make it easy and fun for agents to learn more about you. And you demonstrate a willingness to "put yourself out there" in the way successful authors must do.

2. A healthy presence on social networks. At Web Design Relief (the sister company to Writer's Relief), we emphasize the importance of social media for authors who hope to build an audience. But if you're not a Facebook genius or Twitter virtuoso, don't worry! Simply by maintaining a presence on at least one social network, you can demonstrate to a literary agent that you have the basic building blocks to create a thriving following online.

3. A number of publications in magazines or literary journals. While some authors are able to land great book deals without having a single publishing credit, the majority of authors often have some publications listed in their author bio before they start querying. If you don't have any publications, don't worry.

4. Some experience as a public speaker. While it's not a requirement that you have excellent public speaking skills, it certainly does not hurt if you do. Writers are often asked to speak in public. If your potential agent knows that you are a talented speaker, he or she can use that to your advantage.

5. An interesting personality. These days, publishing houses are relying more and more on the power of social networking to build a writer's fan base. Readers want to like their favorite writer—not just their favorite writer's *books*. If you have a big personality, feel free to show it! But if not, don't worry: There are plenty of quiet, introverted authors who do quite well for themselves.

How Many Fans Do You Need Before Querying A Literary Agent?

Literary agents prefer to see "quality" over "quantity" when it comes to preexisting fans on social networks like Facebook. In other words, having real fans who care about your writing is preferable to having fans who sign up for your Facebook page because they wanted to get something for free.

If you are writing a novel or a memoir, you don't need to worry *too* much about building a vast preexisting fan base. While having a presence online is important, having a *huge* following even before you get out of the gate is not strictly necessary for success. But you do want to establish that you are able to support a fan base. And that means demonstrating that you're willing to make an effort.

How An Author Website Enhances Your Platform

As more and more information moves online, Googleability can make or break a career. Agents, editors, and potential fans will Google you out of curiosity. Be ready for them!

Having an author website shows that you take your role as a writer seriously. It's an invitation for anyone who is interested in your work to get to know you better.

With an author website, you can...

- Be in the right place at the right time...because the Web is open 24/7.
- Integrate your social networks...so friends can become fans.
- Help establish strong branding.
- Make it easier for agents and editors to find and connect with you.
- Give readers an easy way to follow you.
- Showcase your unpublished book or novel.
- Sell your book or novel.
- Showcase your published short stories, essays, or poetry.
- Link to literary journals and magazines (and engage with them).
- Get linked into by online literary journals and other sites.

Here are just a few of the essentials a good author website should showcase to get literary agents excited!

Your Following (or the potential to develop one!)

When visitors to your website like what they see, they'll be more likely to come back. As people become more interested in your writing, they'll comment and participate in discussions. Editors and agents will see a lot of feedback and activity on your site, and they will pick up on the relationship that people have with you and your writing.

Tip: If you've expanded onto social networking sites such as Facebook and Twitter, you can link them to your website to further connect with your audience. (Just make sure you're following social media etiquette if you're going to do this!)

Your Writing Portfolio

Showcasing your works online is a great way to hook literary agents, editors, and fans. IMPORTANT! Be sure you know the rules about previously published writing before you post your words online. By putting up synopses, excerpts, or links to magazines and online literary journals that published your work, you demonstrate that you're on top of your game. Your website is also the place where you can introduce other projects you're working on too!

Reminder: As we've said, literary agents have approached our clients because of a short story or poem published in a literary magazine. Having a website makes it easy for agents—and other key industry players—to find you.

If you're promoting your author website, it's very likely that someone important could read and become intrigued by your work. But if you don't have an author website, it's a bit more difficult for people to connect with you.

Your Web Savviness

By expanding your presence online, you show that you understand how today's world works. Some writers are unenthusiastic about being accessible to readers. But that's not you! How do agents and editors know? Because you have an author website.

If you're writing in one of the commercial genres, your site shows agents and editors that you're capable of promoting yourself and developing a strong "brand."

A Look At The Real You

What inspired you to write? Who are your favorite authors? What made you decide to pursue becoming a published writer?

A query letter bio can only say so much and still fit on one page. But a website has no limits! People visiting your author website hope to get to know the real you. When you give people the details and information they're seeking, you make fans and friends!

Your author website can show literary agents and editors that you're likable, friendly, professional...all the things one hopes for in a partner. So relax, have fun, and be yourself! If your site gives people a good vibe, that energy will carry through into your other endeavors.

If possible, try to work with a website design company that understands the specific needs of creative writers. To get started, you're welcome to check out Web Design Relief (www.WebDesignRelief.com).

Are You Ready To Develop Your Author Platform?

Sign up on www.WebDesignRelief.com to get your free report, *The Writer's Essential Guide To Reputation-Building In A Digital World*, today! We are experts in designing websites specifically for authors. Check it out!

Having a website is an essential strategy; it's no longer optional for serious writers who want to make a name for themselves.

We know what works for author websites. And we're the *best* value on the Web for writers. We know—we did the research. Give us a call today.

Resources On The Writer's Relief Website

Interested in more information about how to improve your writing career? Here are just a few of the many resources on our website!

Submit Write Now! Our weekly e-publication features interviews, news, strategies, tips, publishing leads, contests, and so much more!

Writers Classifieds Pages. Find up-to-the-minute lists of publishing leads, contests, calls for submissions, anthologies, writing conferences, etc.

Publishing Tool Kit. Our tool kit answers just about every question you might have about how to develop a successful submission strategy. Get your tool kit today! Some of the topics include:

- How To Get Published: A Step-By-Step Guide For Beginning And Intermediate Writers
- Grammar And Usage
- Short Story Submissions: How To Submit Short Stories For Publication
- Poetry Submissions: How To Submit Your Poetry For Publication
- Query Letters: Everything You Must Know To Dazzle Literary Agents
- Literary Agent Submissions: How To Find Representation For Your Book Project
- Web Design: Online Marketing And Promotion Strategies For Writers
- Self-Publishing: Everything You Need To Know About Self-Publishing
- How To Handle Rejection: A Writer's Secret Weapon Against Rejection
- Writers Associations: Local And National Organizations For Writers

Video Tutorials. Step-by-step guides for people who aren't sure how to make submissions using email or online submission managers.

Free consultation with a submission strategist. See if Writer's Relief has a plan that will work for your submissions to agents or literary magazines.

Our Invitation To You

Congratulations! You've finished reading our *Field Guide To Literary Agents*!

You now have the tools to connect with and keep a literary agent as you strive to get a book deal. We hope you'll refer to this *Field Guide* whenever you are in need of advice about how to find and work with an agent.

Please reach out to us with your questions or if you need help building a healthy submission strategy.

Keep writing and submitting!

Ronnie L. Smith

Ronnie L. Smith and the Staff of Writer's Relief
www.WritersRelief.com
(866) 405-3003

Every writer suffers the writing blues at some point. And every *successful* writer finds a way through it. Intended for prose and poetry writers alike, *The Happy Writer* offers proven tips and motivational tools to overcome the practical and emotional issues you face as a writer.

You've written short stories, poetry, or essays, and you're ready to get published. What's next? Now you need an effective, long-term submission strategy that gets results. *Publishing Poetry & Prose in Literary Journals* explains everything you need to know—and do—to get your writing published.

More information is available on our website store.

Made in the USA
Monee, IL
13 May 2023

33644450R00079